Murder, Courts, and the Press

Press

Issues in Free Press/Fair Trial

Revised and Expanded Edition

PETER E. KANE

With a Foreword by Franklyn S. Haiman

Southern Illinois University Press

Carbondale and Edwardsville

Library of Congress Cataloging-in-Publication Data

Kane, Peter E., 1932–

    Murder, courts, and the press: issues in free press/fair trial/
Peter E. Kane; with a foreword by Franklyn S. Haiman. —Rev. and
expanded ed.

        p.   cm.

    Includes bibliographical references (p.   ).

    1. Free press and fair trial—United States. 2. Trials (Murder)—
United States. I. Title.
KF9223.5.K36 1992
345.73'056—dc20
[347.30556]
ISBN 0-8093-1780-X   91-40246
ISBN 0-8093-1781-8 (pbk.)   CIP

Contents

Foreword

It has become something of a cliché to assert that the United States has greater freedom of speech and press than any other society in the world has ever enjoyed, but that does not make the observation any the less true. And whether this fact is invoked to defend the status quo and oppose any broader extension of these freedoms, or whether it is offered as a justification for moving even further to eliminate the restrictions that still exist, there is little dispute over the desirability of what we have achieved and its preferability to the alternatives we see in operation around the rest of the globe.

The differences of opinion that we have over whether to maintain or to expand the range of freedom that is available to us are unfortunately too often based on a lack of understanding of what present law and custom actually provide. There are some people, for example, who seem to believe that the First Amendment to the United States Constitution, which says that "Congress shall make no law . . . abridging the freedom of speech, or of the press," means literally that there are no legal limits of any sort on what may be said or printed in our country—thus ignoring the restrictions we have on such forms of expression as obscenity, libel, incitement to riot, or desecration of the flag. There are others, at the opposite extreme, who erroneously seem to think that the government may, consistent with the First Amendment, prohibit whatever a significant number of people find offensive— be it racist rhetoric, the advocacy of communism, or the portrayal of women as objects of sexual exploitation. Before we can intelligently discuss how the balance *ought* to be struck between freedom and restraint, we need to know with accuracy how it currently *is* being struck.

Furthermore, we need to understand the competing interests at stake in any clash between freedom of expression and the limits placed upon it. What harms are alleged to flow from unfettered freedom of speech and press and what purposes are supposedly served by curbing that expression? Unless an overwhelmingly convincing case can be made on behalf of a particular restriction, it is the philosophy of our system of government that expression should remain free and that, where time permits, the remedy for "bad" speech should be more and better speech.

There is probably no area of First Amendment law where the weight of the competing interests which are involved is more equivalent, and the judgment between them more difficult, than in the conflict between freedom of the press and the right to a fair criminal trial. These are, after all, both fundamental rights enshrined in the Constitution, the former in the First Amendment and the latter in the Sixth Amendment, and there are a number of ways in which they are in tension with one another. An unrestricted flow of pretrial publicity about a pending case may make it extremely difficult, if not impossible, to empanel an impartial jury. A media-created circus atmosphere in or around a courtroom may seriously impair the calm, deliberative process that a trial ought to be. The public release of information, such as evidence that is legally inadmissable at the trial, or material that unnecessarily invades the privacy of participants in the litigation, may also undermine the integrity of the process with perhaps little or no countervailing justification. Because this contest of rights is such a close one, a sophisticated examination of the issue of free press versus fair trial is an exercise that is not only valuable in its own right but also for the illumination it sheds on other difficult First Amendment problems where closely competing interests have to be adjudicated.

Thus this book by Peter Kane provides us, not only with a

fascinating set of problem cases which challenge us to explore the free press/fair trial question in depth, but also with a useful tool for heightening our awareness and developing our analytic skills with regard to problems in freedom of expression generally. One can immerse oneself, perhaps to good purpose, in reading theoretical treatises on freedom of expression, but until one begins to apply those theories and principles to concrete cases, involving real human beings and actual human events, one has not completed the task of becoming educated about the First Amendment.

Because of the dramatic quality of the material with which *Murder, Courts, and the Press* deals, this book is an excellent hors d'oeurve for whetting the appetite of people newly arrived at an interest in freedom of expression and enticing them on to the full course dinners that other, broader treatments of First Amendment issues provide. If it does nothing more than serve that purpose it will have played a valuable role But its potential is far greater than that, for it may also contribute significantly to the wiser resolution of the particular issue of free press versus fair trial with which our courts are struggling every day.

Franklyn S. Haiman
Northwestern University

Preface to Revised and Expanded Edition

Events since the publication of the first edition of this book in 1986 have demonstrated the enduring nature of the tension in the United States between the First Amendment right of a free press and a criminal defendant's Sixth Amendment right to a fair trial. While the first edition was in press, Claus von Bülow's second trial for attempted murder took place and was one of the media events of our time. The incidence of serial killing seems to be more prevalent, or at least there is greater public exposure to the special horrors of these crimes. Murder, murder investigations, and murder trials continue to hold a fascination for the public.

The preparation of a revised and expanded edition of this book has provided an opportunity to consider two topics that were not discussed in the first edition—cameras in the courtroom and a code of ethics for crime reporting. The second Claus von Bülow attempted-murder trial with its live television broadcast by the Cable News Network provides a good example for consideration of the first issue. The massive pretrial reporting in the Rochester, New York, area about Arthur Shawcross and the multiple murders he committed presents an excellent case study for consideration of the second issue. In addition, errors have been corrected, thoughts left unclear and/or incomplete have been explained and expanded, and references have been added to the case list and bibliography.

· While the press continues to respond to the real or perceived public interest in murders, the courts seem to be more concerned than ever for the defendant's fair trial rights. Even in cases such as *Shawcross,* discussed in chapter 8, where the guilt of the defendant is not really in doubt, lawyers and judges still seem to make a real effort to secure an impartial jury. Defense lawyers can be vigorous in their pursuit of every possible means to deal with prejudicial publicity.

One problem that arises in all litigation is that of expenses. Skilled and successful defense lawyers do not come cheap, and it is generally only the very rich who can afford their services. On the other hand, it is usually only the alleged crimes of the rich (or in which the rich are victims) that generate the kind of pretrial publicity that requires heroic legal defense efforts. Claus von Bülow can counteract extensive prejudicial news reports by hiring the best legal defense staff available. In contrast there is little public interest in the average crimes of the poor and unknown and thus little or no reporting on these cases.

While there might appear to be a rough balance between pretrial publicity and the means to mount a vigorous defense, such is not always the case. Within the community from which his jury would be chosen, Arthur Shawcross was the subject of prejudicial pretrial publicity fully as extensive as that which Claus von Bülow received. But Shawcross with no money was represented at his trial by the public defender. While many of these defenders are excellent trial lawyers, none has neither the time nor the resources to do the extensive background work that would be expected of a wealthy client's private practice lawyer. The difficulties are particularly great for those defendants who are the victims of ongoing prejudice because of their race, ethnic background, sexual orientation, or any other characteristic that places them in a despised minority group.

In a long view, the system that has developed to balance the rights of a free press and to a fair trial seems to work fairly well. However, that long view is of little comfort to the defendant in a particular case in which the system breaks down owing to the excessive zeal of the press or a prosecutor or the incompetence of a judge or defense lawyer. In a recent article in the *American University Law Review* Newton Minow and Fred Cate review a large number of studies of the effectiveness of the many widely used remedies for prejudicial publicity that are discussed in the pages that follow. The general conclusion is that these remedies do not work very well. Since there is no constitutional way to limit press reporting on criminal cases, Minow and Cate argue that impartial jurors are able to set aside any adverse influence that news reports might generate. However, given the frequency of cases in which community prejudices are inflamed by news reports and the activities of parties to the case, the selection of impartial jury is probably more difficult than ever.

Preface to First Edition

With the exception of dedicated lawyers and scholars, most people find law in general and constitutional law in particular to be a dry and boring subject. Appreciative reading of the often tedious and turgid prose of opinions from appellate courts and the United States Supreme Court requires special interest and commitment. The chore of deciphering the frequently tortucus logic of an opinion obscures the fact that the writer of the opinion is dealing with a real case involving the real problems of real human beings. This reality is too often lost in legal abstractions.

Occasionally an opinion comes along that breaks through the abstractions to present the reader with the reality. Such an opinion is that of Justice Tom Clark in the case of *Sheppard v. Maxwell*. In *Sheppard*, Justice Clark explained and defended the decision of the United States Supreme Court by presenting his readers with a detailed account of the events in Sam Sheppard's murder trial showing that Sheppard did not receive a fair trial.

Reading Justice Clark's *Sheppard* opinion led me to ask why the study of constitutional law could not always be this interesting. What follows is my attempt to answer that question in the affirmative in the area of free press/fair trial controversies. For most of the cases considered in this volume readers will find that opinions have been written by justices of the United States Supreme Court. Except for the Clark opinion, readers of these opinions will never clearly perceive that the justices are writing about real people and events. While it is important to understand the legal principles in these opinions, it would also seem important to understand the realities of the cases. In the final analysis the abstract legalities only have meaning within the context of the real world.

For the cases considered in this volume I have attempted to produce a comprehensive understanding by combining a description of the realities of the cases with an analysis of the opinions of the United States Supreme Court designed to explain the legal principles embedded in those opinions. If this narrative and analysis approach works as intended, general readers will find interesting stories that lead to an understanding of legal principles, and students of constitutional law will broaden their appreciation of the realities that underlie the abstractions of court opinions.

In our system of government two of the most important safeguards of our freedom are the courts and the press. A secure and free society must perceive that its legal system is operating fairly and that justice is in fact being done. The press serves us by reporting on the activities of the legal system and government in general so that we who are supposed to be the ultimate decision makers in our system of government have the information needed to make those decisions. One of the elements that made the scandals that came to bear the label "Watergate" so reprehensible was the deliberate efforts by the president of the United States and others to subvert both courts and press. When the legal system resisted these attacks and eventually did work, a waning public faith in that system was restored. The press in this case can be both praised and criticized—praised for first revealing what some of the scandal might be and criticized for in most part printing government handouts and failing to undertake adequate independent investigations of the situation. Of course it must be recognized that efforts by the press to perform its job were consistently undermined by an administration bent on keeping its illegal and unethical conduct secret. Even today the public does not know the full extent of the Nixon administration abuses because a substantial portion of the documents that would reveal the whole story are still withheld from public view through the legal and political efforts of many of those whose possible misdeeds might be exposed. Clearly the "Watergate" scandal demonstrates why it is important that we understand something of the functioning of both courts and press.

Free press and fair trial is a subject area that offers a good introduction to the study of principles of freedom of expression, the legal process, and journalistic practices. Crime stories have traditionally been the journalist's bread and butter, and sensational crime stories can make both headlines and reputations. These are also often the stories that a curious public demands. In fact, newer and juicier and more detailed crime stories serve everyone's interests except, perhaps, the persons accused of the crime. There is no doubt that in the drive to get the story that will attract listeners, readers, or viewers the interests of the accused are given little or no consideration. Journalistic codes of conduct are often ignored in the pursuit of a good story. The narratives that follow present opportunities to ask what the proper conduct of journalists should be.

In other countries such as Great Britain perceived excesses (both actual and imagined) in the gathering and dissemination of news are dealt with by strict laws and court orders. In the United States the First Amendment to our Constitution has been interpreted as a prohibition on interference with journalistic activity in the area of crime reporting. Thus our freedom to communicate creates a problem to be resolved since the evidence is clear that this freedom can and does undermine another constitutional right—the Sixth Amendment right to a fair trial. Resolution of this apparent conflict of rights requires sophisticated and imaginative approaches. At times judges find appropriate techniques, and at other times techniques have been used that the United States Supreme Court has found wanting. Dealing with freedom in general and freedom of communication in particular is not a simple task. There are few easy answers.

The narratives of this volume also provide an introduction to the operation of the courts in the area of criminal justice. The trial court is the arena in which the conflicts between a free press and a fair trial are played out. This play is described here as are the subsequent evaluations of that play by the appellate courts. Thus the legal process is considered from its beginning with the original crime to the final resolution of the case in the United States Supreme Court.

Finally, I have included a special section that presents a very specific area of direct conflict between the courts and journalists. Circumstances occasionally create a situation in which a judge feels compelled to order a journalist to do something that the journalist feels compelled not to do. Here the two forces meet head on. The journalist appears to assert that a free press (as defined by the journalist) is of greater importance in our society than a fair trial. The judge makes just the opposite claim. These instances offer still additional insights into the problems of freedom of expression, the legal process, and the practices of journalists.

In sum, what I have done here is to bring together a group of interesting murder case stories that will both entertain and inform. These cases, dealing as they do with freedom of expression and the proper functioning of the legal system—two elements extremely important to our political processes, have value beyond their ability to entertain. Freedom of expression, a right that we too often take for granted, is not an area of simple absolutes but is frequently one of problems and conflicts that need to be resolved. These cases introduce those problems and conflicts. The proper functioning of the legal system depends at least in part on the discretionary power of trial court judges. These cases demonstrate some of the extent of and limits to that discretion and illustrate how various judges have used or abused their power. Insight is also provided into the power and practices of journalists—the uses and abuses of journalistic endeavor.

Murder, Courts, and The Press

CHAPTER 1

An Introduction to the Problem

One path to an improved understanding of the past is the study of the official documents that were produced by people in their time. Charters, constitutions, laws, and the like reflect the concerns of the members of the society that produced these documents. For example, the largest portion of the Declaration of Independence contains a list of abuses by King George III of Great Britain that the American colonists were presenting to the world to explain and justify their rebellion. A reading of these charges discloses the many ways that the British government interfered with the executive, judicial, and legislative functions of government in the colonies. The document also lists violations of civil liberties—violations of the fundamental rights of Englishmen claimed by the colonists. Among these violations are the denial of trial by jury and the shipping of accused persons to England to stand trial.

The kinds of colonial experiences that led to the American Revolution are again reflected in the catalog of civil liberties guarantees contained in the first ten amendments to the Constitution known as the Bill of Rights, adopted in 1791, fifteen years after the Declaration of Independence. For example, the British tried to maintain control by disarming and disbanding colonial military groups. Thus the Second Amendment guarantees to the former colonies, now states, the right to maintain an armed militia. The British reduced military expenses by housing soldiers in private homes where they were expected to be fed, too. Thus the Third Amendment prohibits this practice. British officers would break into homes and seize property without cause. Thus the Fourth Amendment requires law officers to secure a warrant prior to conducting a search or seizing property. The British often held colonists without charge and even took their possessions and property without any legal authority to do so. Thus the Fifth Amendment requires legal due process and the right to an indictment in major criminal cases.

For the purposes of this study two articles of the Bill of Rights are important. During the colonial era the British, and some colonial assemblies as well, attempted to prevent unfavorable publicity through tight control of the press and to punish through fines and imprisonment any unfavorable comment that did appear. The Bill of Rights recognizes the central role of free expression in a free society by guaranteeing freedom of speech and press. A reader of the First Amendment must be impressed by the striking, absolute nature of the statement of this guarantee. "Congress shall make no law . . . abridging the freedom of speech, or of the press; . . ."

A second major colonial problem was that of securing a fair trial for those accused of crimes. A source of special dissatisfaction was the treatment of those accused of smuggling. Because of the levels of taxation and restrictions on commerce imposed by England, many colonists dealt with untaxed and other forms of contraband goods. The English responded with vigorous efforts to enforce their laws through the search for and seizure of contraband and through the prosecution of those suspected of dealing in contraband. For the accused the process of prosecution was in itself an overwhelming ordeal. A suspect was often held for an extended period of time before being shipped to England to stand trial before an Admiralty Court. Even after he was delivered to England, he might spend a lengthy time in jail before being brought to trial. The trial itself was usually held in a closed court. The proceedings of the court were not made public, and occasionally even the judgments of the court were not publicly announced.

One response to the injustice of this English system of trial is found in the specific requirements for a fair trial listed in the Sixth Amendment to the Constitution. This amendment says in part, "the accused shall enjoy the right to a speedy and public trial, by an impartial jury of the State and district wherein the crime shall have been committed."

While these guarantees represent a substantial improvement over eighteenth-century English practices, many problems arise from the effort to assure simultaneously all these rights. For example, in the case of a crime that attracts a great deal of public attention, it may be difficult if not impossible to find an "impartial" jury at a time and place close to that crime. The most common solution to this problem in the average case is that of waiver by the accused of his rights to time and place proximity in order to assure jury impartiality. In technical terms the accused asks for a continuance to delay the trial or a change of venue, which is a request that the trial be moved to some other locality, or both.

While a prompt trial before a jury of one's neighbors provides reasonable assurance of fair treatment in most cases, the occasional exceptions demand attention because of their special character. The average criminal trial is of little interest to the general public and attracts little attention. The occasional exceptions are the cases in which the nature of the crime, the fame of the victim, or the notoriety of the accused excites public imagination. For example, people are eager to hear about murders that are particularly gruesome or involve sexual matters, robberies of very large amounts of money, a celebrity's loss of jewelry, or a renowned financier's indictment for tax evasion. The public appetite for information is both satisfied and further stimulated by the news media for whom the supplying of this information is profitable. The profit element can, in fact, create a situation in which media outlets compete with one another to see who can supply the most, the newest, or the best materials. The unpopular defendant or the person accused of a particularly heinous crime may also be the subject of critical and judgmental statements by the news media.

If a defendant is to have a fair trial, he is entitled to have his case heard by an unprejudiced jury composed of individuals who have not formed an opinion regarding his guilt and who will form their opinion only on the evidence presented to them in court. For the defendant in the exceptional case, these conditions can be difficult and perhaps impossible to meet. A change in the location of a trial may be of little help in particularly notorious cases. If passions have been particularly inflamed, anything less than an indefinite delay may not be adequate.

A good example of this problem is the case of John Hinckley Jr.'s trial for shooting President Ronald Reagan. Shooting the president of the United States is an infamous act that is sure to receive the widest publicity. In this case the act was observed and recorded by television news cameramen, and these videotapes in slow motion and living color were shown repeatedly on just about every television outlet in the country and many others throughout the world. How could an "impartial" jury be selected when it was probably impossible to find twelve people who had not seen Hinckley's attack on television?

The problem of everyone as eyewitness to the event is compounded by the follow-up stories provided by the news media to a curious public. These stories gave detailed biographies of the suspect, extended analyses of his psychological state, and lengthy discussions and comments about Hinckley's affection for movie actress Jody Foster as the motive for his actions. Thus, not only had the jurors seen the crime, but also they were probably intimately familiar with the life, loves, and fantasies of the accused.

In order to serve impartially a juror must somehow set aside all that has been seen and heard about the case prior to trial.

One solution to the problems created by the exceptional case is to control or limit the information which the public can receive. In Great Britain news media are forbidden to publish anything more than the simple facts of a crime and arrest. In reporting on a trial they may publish only the information that is presented in court. However, in the United States efforts to establish and enforce similar rules have consistently been rejected by the Supreme Court as violations of the First Amendment guarantee of freedom of the press. For several years the American Bar Association has been considering rules to achieve similar results in a different way. This proposal would place a limit on the types of information either side in a criminal case could supply to the news media.

If the damage of extensive or prejudicial information cannot be avoided, appellate courts have sometimes taken the necessary steps to see that a possible injustice is corrected. Convictions in trials held in clearly prejudiced circumstances can be set aside and new trials ordered. The process of appeal itself means that the new trial will occur after a substantial delay. In addition, these rulings may order a change of venue so that the new trial will be held in a different locality. This solution is, however, only an expedient in a particular case. The fundamental conflict between the news media's right to publish and the public's right to know on the one hand and the right of the criminal accused to a fair trial before an impartial and unprejudiced jury has not yet been satisfactorily resolved.

What follows is a review of seven criminal cases since 1954 in which the courts of this country have attempted to address the problem of balancing the rights guaranteed by the First Amendment with those guaranteed by the Sixth Amendment. The cases range from those in which the United States Supreme Court found violations of the fair trial rights of the accused, to those where

the Supreme Court found First Amendment violations, to those
in which the trial judge was found to have struck a proper balance
between these seemingly conflicting constitutional guarantees.
While all seven of these cases happen to be murder cases (perhaps
because this dramatic crime attracts the most public attention)
the basis for selection has not been the nature of the crime but
rather the way in which the cases illuminate important facets of
the free press/fair trial controversy. Because each of these seven
cases (like all free press/fair trial confrontations) is a real life
situation and not just an abstraction for the consideration of legal
scholars, the circumstances of the original crime and prosecution
will be described in detail. These descriptions are designed to
help the reader understand the real dynamics of the seeming
conflicts between the First and Sixth Amendments.

of *The Press*, followed with a front page editorial on July 20 headlined "Getting Away With Murder." The editorial suggested that the police were not really trying to develop a case because of the status of the prime suspect. The two other Cleveland papers, *The News* and the *Plain Dealer*, joined in editorial comment critical of the police and Dr. Sam Sheppard.

The influence of editorial comment on the case can be clearly shown. On July 21, *The Press* ran an editorial entitled, "Why No Inquest? Do It Now, Dr. Gerber," and the coroner, Dr. Sam Gerber, called an inquest that same day. The atmosphere of the inquest has been effectively described by United States Supreme Court Justice Tom Clark in his opinion for the eight-justice majority in Sheppard v. Maxwell, 384 U.S. 333, rendered in 1966.

> A swarm of reporters and photographers attended. Sheppard was brought into the room by police who searched him in full view of several hundred spectators. Sheppard's counsel were present during the three-day inquest but were not permitted to participate. When Sheppard's chief counsel attempted to place some documents in the record, he was forcibly ejected from the room by the Coroner, who received cheers, hugs, and kisses from ladies in the audience. Sheppard was questioned for five and one-half hours about his actions on the night of the murder, his married life, and a love affair with Susan Hayes. At the end of the hearing the Coroner announced that he "could" order Sheppard held for the grand jury, but did not do so.

Within a week Seltzer's patience again expired, and *The Press* ran a front page editorial on July 30, with the headline, "Why Isn't Sam Sheppard in Jail." In later editions the headline was changed to "Quit Stalling Bring Him In." In boldface caps the editorial said in part:

police. He examined Marilyn Sheppard and determined that she was in fact dead. He also examined Sam and, with the help of the police at the scene, placed Sam in his station wagon and took him to the Bay View Hospital. Examination at the hospital indicated that Sam was suffering from shock, had been beaten around the face and head, and had possibly sustained a broken neck. Although subsequent examination showed that his spinal injury was less severe, Dr. Sheppard wore a leather neck brace throughout the course of the investigation and subsequent trial.

From the outset Dr. Sam was apparently the prime suspect in the case. There were no clues regarding the burly man other than Sheppard's vague description. In addition the investigation of the case soon brought to light possible motives for the crime. Mrs. Sheppard was vaguely linked romantically with a neighbor, and there was considerable gossip about Dr. Sam's relations with a number of patients. Finally, Susan Hayes, a laboratory technician formerly employed at the hospital, was found, and she admitted having an affair with Sheppard. A thorough examination of both Sheppard and his home failed to turn up any physical evidence to link him to the crime. Extensive questioning of Sheppard was also unproductive.

It is quite natural that the murder of Marilyn Sheppard would attract the attention of the press. The crime, investigation, and trial that followed was extensively covered not only in the Cleveland papers but also in major papers throughout the country. The only real exception to the exuberant coverage of the case was *The New York Times*, which carried the story but relegated it to the depths of the inside pages. After the investigation by several different law enforcement groups had dragged on without clear results for some two weeks, the tone of treatment of the story by the Cleveland newspapers changed. *The Press* wrote a critical editorial suggesting that the law enforcement agencies involved in the case should make coordinate efforts in the interest of justice. The next day such a meeting was held. Louis Seltzer, editor practice. He served as police surgeon for the community and, as his early morning call indicated, was at least a fairly close friend of the village mayor.

The only available witness to the events of the night of July 4 was Samuel Sheppard. He reported that after a hectic day's work at the hospital he had fallen asleep on the couch while watching the late movie on television. He was later aroused from his sleep enough to be aware that his wife had gone upstairs to bed. Still later something, possibly a scream, awakened him. and he rushed upstairs to the bedroom. He sensed the presence of someone else in the bedroom just before he was struck a blow from behind and knocked unconscious. When he regained consciousness, he discovered his wife's body, checked her pulse to determine she was dead, and went to his son's room where he found that the boy was all right and still asleep. Sheppard reported that he then heard a noise downstairs which he investigated. He spotted a burly man with bushy hair whom he chased out of the house and down to the beach. The two men struggled briefly, and Sheppard was again knocked out. He awoke lying face down on the sand with the lower half of his body in the water. He returned to the house, checked his wife's pulse once more, and called Mayor Houk.

Other evidence added very little to the Sheppard account. A witness reported that the lights were on in the Sheppard house at about 2:15 A.M. The police investigation discovered no unidentified fingerprints but did discover that effort had been made to clean up a trail of blood that extended downstairs from the bedroom. In addition someone had apparently tried to clean up blood using the basement sink. The coroner concluded that Mrs. Sheppard's death had been due to blows from an object such as a golf club. The murder weapon was never found. There was no evidence of a forced entry.

After Mayor Houk called the police, he called Sam's brother Richard who arrived at the Sam Sheppard house shortly after the

CHAPTER 2

Sins of Commission and Omission
The Sheppard Murder Case

The fashionable suburban community of Bay Village, Ohio, is located on the shores of Lake Erie about twenty miles west of downtown Cleveland. In Bay Village on the night of July 4, 1954, Marilyn Sheppard was beaten to death in her upstairs bedroom of the Sheppard's lakefront home by person or persons unknown. Although an autopsy placed the time of death between 3:00 and 4:00 A.M., the crime was first reported at 5:50 A.M. when the victim's husband, Dr. Samuel Sheppard, called his friend and neighbor J. Spencer Houk, the mayor of Bay Village. Mr. and Mrs. Houk hurried to the Sheppard house, discovered what had happened, and called the village police. Marilyn Sheppard was four months pregnant at the time of her death.

Dr. Samuel Sheppard was an osteopathic physician who practiced with his father and two brothers in Bay Village. The four Sheppards owned and operated the 300-bed Bay View Hospital in the town. Sam and Marilyn Sheppard had been childhood sweethearts. They were married in 1945 and had one child, Sam Jr. ("Chip"), who was six at the time of the murder. In 1951 the Sheppards returned to Bay Village, and Dr. Sam joined the family practice. Like his father and brothers, he quickly assumed a position of prestige and prominence within the community and had all the financial benefits that accrue from a successful medical

THIS IS MURDER. THIS IS NO PARLOR GAME. THIS IS NO TIME TO PERMIT ANYBODY—NO MATTER WHO HE IS—TO OUTWIT, STALL, FAKE, OR IMPROVISE DEVICES TO KEEP AWAY FROM THE POLICE OR FROM THE QUESTIONING ANYBODY IN HIS RIGHT MIND KNOWS A MURDER SUSPECT SHOULD BE SUBJECTED TO—AT A POLICE STATION.

That evening Sam Sheppard was arrested and arraigned in the presence of a multitude of newsmen who apparently knew in advance of the arrest. He was held in jail and indicted for murdering his wife by a grand jury on August 17.

Publicity concerning the *Sheppard* case was continuous from the time the crime was originally reported. There was no letup after either the arrest or indictment. The circumstances immediately prior to the trial and the conditions under which the trial was held were also described by Justice Clark.

With this background the case came on for trial two weeks before the November general election at which the chief prosecutor was a candidate for common pleas judge and the trial judge, Judge Blythin, was a candidate to succeed himself. Twenty-five days before the case was set, 75 veniremen were called as prospective jurors. All three Cleveland newspapers published the names and addresses of the veniremen. As a consequence, anonymous letters and telephone calls, as well as calls from friends, regarding the impending prosecution were received by all of the prospective jurors. The selection of the jury began on October 18, 1954.

The courtroom in which the trial was held measured 26 by 48 feet. A long temporary table was set up inside the bar, in back of the single counsel table. It ran the width of the courtroom, parallel to the bar railing, with one end less than three feet from the jury box. Approximately 20 representatives of newspapers and wire services were assigned seats at this table by the court. Behind the bar railing there were four rows of benches. These seats were likewise assigned by the court for the entire trial. The first row was occupied by representatives of television and radio stations, and the second and third rows by reporters from out-of-town newspapers and magazines. One side of the last row, which accommodated 14 people, was assigned to Sheppard's family and the other to Marilyn's. . . .

. . . The courtroom remained crowded to capacity with representatives of news media. Their movement in and out of the courtroom often caused so much confusion that, despite the loud-speaker system installed in the courtroom, it was difficult for the witnesses and counsel to be heard. Furthermore, the reporters clustered within the bar of the small courtroom made confidential talk among Sheppard and his counsel almost impossible during the proceedings. They frequently had to leave the courtroom to obtain privacy. And many times when counsel wished to raise a point with the judge out of the hearing of the jury it was necessary to move to the judge's chambers. Even then, news media representatives so packed the judge's anteroom that counsel could hardly return from the chambers to the courtroom. The reporters vied with each other to find out what counsel and the judge had discussed, and often these matters later appeared in newspapers accessible to the jury. . . .

The jurors themselves were constantly exposed to the news media. Every juror, except one, testified at *voir dire* [the questioning of prospective jurors] to reading about the case in the Cleveland papers or to having heard broadcasts about it. Seven of the 12 jurors who rendered the verdict had one or more Cleveland papers delivered in their home; the remaining jurors were not interrogated on the point.

. . . During the trial, pictures of the jury appeared over 40 times in the Cleveland papers alone. The court permitted photographers to take pictures of the jury in the box, and individual pictures of the members in the jury room.

As he developed his opinion in *Sheppard v. Maxwell*, Justice Clark presented a catalog of examples of news media conduct during the course of the trial and the ways in which trial Judge Edward Blythin dealt with this conduct. The following four examples from that listing are illustrative of the problems that arose.

(1) On November 19, a Cleveland police officer gave testimony that tended to contradict details in the written statement Sheppard made to the Cleveland police. Two days later, in a broadcast heard over Station WHK in Cleveland, Robert Considine likened Sheppard to a perjurer and compared the episode to Alger Hiss' confrontation with Whitaker Chambers. Though defense counsel asked the judge to question the jury to ascertain how many heard the broadcast, the court refused to do so. The judge also overruled the motion for continuance based on the same ground, saying:

"Well, I don't know, we can't stop people, in any event, listening to it. It is a matter of free speech, and the court can't control everybody. . . We are not going to harass the jury every morning. . . . It is getting to the point where if we do it every morning, we are suspecting the jury. I have confidence in this jury. . . ."

(2) On November 24, a story appeared under an eight-column headline: "Sam Called A 'Jekyll-Hyde' by Marilyn, Cousin to Testify." It related that Marilyn had recently told friends that Sheppard was a "Dr. Jekyll and Mr. Hyde" character. No such testimony was ever produced at the trial. The story went on to announce: "the prosecution has a

'bombshell witness' on tap who will testify to Dr. Sam's display of fiery temper—countering with the defense claim that the defendant is a gentle physician with an even disposition." Defense counsel made motions for a change of venue, continuance and mistrial, but they were denied. No action was taken by the court.

(3) When the trial was in its seventh week, Walter Winchell broadcast over WXEL television and WJW radio that Carole Beasley, who was under arrest in New York City for robbery, had stated that, as Sheppard's mistress, she had borne him a child. The defense asked that the jury be queried on the broadcast. Two jurors admitted in open court that they had heard it. The judge asked each: "Would that have any effect on your judgment?" Both replied, "No." This was accepted by the judge as sufficient; he merely asked the jury to "pay no attention whatever to that type of scavenging. . . . Let's confine ourselves to this courtroom, if you please." In answer to the motion for mistrial, the judge said:

"Well, even, so, Mr. Corrigan, how are you ever going to prevent those things, in any event? I don't justify them at all. I think it is outrageous, but in a sense, it is outrageous even if there were no trial here. The trial has nothing to do with it in the Court's mind, as far as its outrage is concerned, but—"

Mr. Corrigan: I don't know what effect it had on the mind of any of these jurors, and I cannot find out unless inquiry is made.

The Court: How would you ever, in any jury, avoid that kind of a thing?

(4) On December 9, while Sheppard was on the witness stand he testified that he had been mistreated by Cleveland detectives after his arrest. Although he was not at the trial, Captain Kerr of the Homicide Bureau issued a press state-

ment denying Sheppard's allegations which appeared under the headline: " 'Bare-faced Liar,' Kerr Says of Sam." Captain Kerr never appeared as a witness at the trial.

After almost two months the trial was completed, and the case was handed to the jury. During the jury's deliberations, it was for the first time sequestered (secluded from public contact). This technique, now frequently used in trials that attract much public attention, involves confining the jury in special quarters where the members have no chance to talk to any outsiders about the case or to be exposed to any information other than that which is presented in court. The jury considered the case for five days and, on December 21, found Sam Sheppard guilty of murder in the second degree. Judge Blythin immediately sentenced Sheppard to life imprisonment—the maximum possible sentence for this crime. Questions about Judge Blythin's impartiality were undercored by the revelation ten years after the trial by Dorothy Kilgallen, one of the famous reporters who covered the trial, that the judge had said to her, "It's an open and shut case . . . he is guilty as hell." Because by then Judge Blythin had been dead for several years, his side of this story was never presented.

It was not until 1966, twelve years after Samuel Sheppard's trial and conviction, that the United States Supreme Court considered the case and rendered a decision that voided Sheppard's conviction. The basis for this action was stated by Justice Clark in the concluding portions of the Court's written opinion.

There can be no question about the nature of the publicity which surrounded Sheppard's trial.

Indeed, every court that has considered this case, save the court that tried it, has deplored the manner in which the news media inflamed and prejudiced the public.

Much of the material printed or broadcast during the trial was never heard from the witness stand, such as the charges that Sheppard had purposely impeded the murder investigation and must be guilty since he had hired a prominent criminal lawyer; that Sheppard was a perjurer; that he had sexual relations with numerous women; that his slain wife had characterized him as a "Jekyll-Hyde"; that he was "a bare-faced liar" because of his testimony as to police treatment; and finally, that a woman convict claimed Sheppard to be the father of her illegitimate child. As the trial progressed, the newspapers summarized and interpreted the evidence, devoting particular attention to the material that incriminated Sheppard, and often drew unwarranted inferences from testimony.

Nor is there any doubt that this deluge of publicity reached at least some of the jury. On the only occasion that the jury was queried, two jurors admitted in open court to hearing the highly inflammatory charge that a prison inmate claimed Sheppard as the father of her illegitimate child.

The court's fundamental error is compounded by the holding that it lacked power to control the publicity about the trial. From the very inception of the proceedings the judge announced that neither he nor anyone else could restrict prejudicial news accounts. And he reiterated this view on numerous occasions. Since he viewed the news media as his target, the judge never considered other means that are often utilized to reduce the appearance of prejudicial material and to protect the jury from outside influence. . . .

The carnival atmosphere at trial could easily have been avoided since the courtroom and courthouse premises are subject to the control of the court. . . . Bearing in mind the massive pretrial publicity, the judge should have adopted stricter rules governing the use of the courtroom by newsmen, as Sheppard's counsel requested. The number of reporters in the courtroom itself could have been limited at the first sign that their presence would disrupt the trial. They certainly should not have been placed inside the bar. Furthermore, the judge should have more closely regulated the conduct of newsmen in the courtroom. For instance, the judge belatedly asked them not to handle and photograph trial exhibits lying on the counsel table during the recesses.

Secondly, the court should have insulated the witnesses. All of the newspapers and radio stations apparently interviewed prospective witnesses at will, and in many instances disclosed their testimony. A typical example was the publication of numerous statements by Susan Hayes, before her appearance in court, regarding her love affair with Sheppard. Although the witnesses were barred from the courtroom during the trial the full verbatim testimony was available to them in the press. This completely nullified the judge's imposition of the rule.

Thirdly, the court should have made some effort to control the release of leads, information, and gossip to the press by police officers, witnesses, and the counsel for both sides. Much of the information thus disclosed was inaccurate, leading to groundless rumors and confusion. That the judge was aware of his responsibility in this respect may be seen from his warning to Steve Sheppard, the accused's brother, who had apparently made public statements in an attempt to discredit testimony for the prosecution. The judge made this statement in the presence of the jury:

"Now, the Court wants to say a word. That he was told—he has not read anything about it at all—but he was informed that Dr. Steve Sheppard, who has been granted the privilege of remaining in the court room during the trial, has been trying the case in the newspapers and making rather uncomplimentary comments about the testimony of the witnesses for the State.

"Let it be now understood that if Dr. Steve Sheppard

wishes to use the newspapers to try his case while we are
trying it here, he will be barred from remaining in the
court room during the progress of the trial if he is to be a
witness in the case.

"The Court appreciates he cannot deny Steve Sheppard
the right of free speech, but he can deny him the . . .
privilege of being in the court room, if he wants to avail
himself of that method during the progress of the trial."

Defense counsel immediately brought to the court's attention the tremendous amount of publicity in the Cleveland press that "misrepresented entirely the testimony" in
the case. Under such circumstances, the judge should have
at least warned the newspapers to check the accuracy of
their accounts. And it is obvious that the judge should have
further sought to alleviate this problem by imposing control
over the statements made to the news media by counsel,
witnesses, and especially the Coroner and police officers.
The prosecution repeatedly made evidence available to the
news media which was never offered in the trial. Much of
the "evidence" disseminated in this fashion was clearly inadmissible. The exclusion of such evidence in court is rendered meaningless when news media make it available to
the public. For example, the publicity about Sheppard's refusal to take a lie detector test came directly from police
officers and the coroner. The story that Sheppard had been
called a "Jekyll-Hyde" personality by his wife was attributed to a prosecution witness. No such testimony was
given.

The further report that there was "a 'bombshell witness'
on tap" who would testify as to Sheppard's "fiery temper"
could only have emanated from the prosecution. Moreover,
the newspapers described in detail clues that have been
found by the police, but not put into the record.

The fact that many of the prejudicial news items can be

traced to the prosecution, as well as the defense, aggravates
the judge's failure to take any action. Effective control of
these sources—concededly within the court's power—
might well have prevented the divulgence of inaccurate information, rumors, and accusations that made up much of
the inflammatory publicity, at least after Sheppard's
indictment.

More specifically, the trial court might well have pros-
cribed extra-judicial statements by any lawyer, party, witness, or court official which divulged prejudicial matters
such as the refusal of Sheppard to submit to interrogation or
take any lie detector tests; any statement made by Sheppard
to officials; the identity of prospective witnesses or their
probable testimony; any belief in guilt or innocence; or like
statements concerning the merits of the case. Being advised
of the great public interest in the case, the mass coverage of
the press, and the potential prejudicial impact of publicity,
the court could also have requested the appropriate city and
county officials to promulgate a regulation with respect to
dissemination of information about the case by their employees. In addition, reporters who wrote or broadcast prejudicial stories, could have been warned as to the
impropriety of publishing material not introduced in the
proceedings.

The judge was put on notice of such events by defense
counsel's complaint about the WHK broadcast on the second day of the trial. In this manner, Sheppard's right to a
trial free from outside interference would have been given
added protection without corresponding curtailment of the
news media. Had the judge, the other officers of the court,
and the police placed the interest of justice first, the news
media would have soon learned to be content with the task
of reporting the case as it unfolded in the courtroom—not
pieced together from extrajudicial statements. . . .

Since the state trial judge did not fulfill his duty to protect Sheppard from the inherently prejudicial publicity
which saturated the community and to control disruptive
influences in the courtroom, we must reverse the denial of
the habeas petition. The case is remanded to the District
Court with instructions to issue the writ and order that
Sheppard be released from custody unless the State puts
him to its charges again within a reasonable time.

When Samuel Sheppard was retried under rigorously con-
trolled circumstances, he was acquitted.

The case of Samuel Sheppard illustrates the failure of the trial
judge, whatever his motives might have been, to make use of the
techniques available to him in the law to provide the defendant
with a fair trial. Justice Clark in his opinion for the majority of
the United States Supreme Court reviewed those techniques.

1. Through his attorney Sam Sheppard stated his willingness
to waive his Sixth Amendment right to a speedy trial in the place
where the crime was committed. Judge Blythin denied these requests for a continuance and/or change of venue. The result was
that the trial was held at election time in the place where principal
actors in the trial, including the judge, were running for office.
Regardless of the political climate as seen in this case, trial courts
are generally reluctant to grant defendant requests for continuance or change of venue, and appellate courts have ruled in a
number of cases that the trial judge was in error for failing to
grant these requests, particularly in circumstances such as the
Sheppard case.

2. Proper caution was not taken to assure that Sam Sheppard
had an impartial jury. The first step in this process should have
been a more extensive examination of potential jurors, the voir
dire examination, to make sure that those finally selected to serve
on the jury had not been influenced by the pretrial publicity. In
light of the continued publicity concerning this case, the judge

could have taken the more drastic step of ordering the jury to be sequestered. This step would have meant that the jury would be kept under guard, fed and housed at some hotel at public expense, and forbidden to see or hear any news about the case until the trial was over. A simple and less drastic step would have been to order the jurors to avoid all contact with news media reports.

3. As Justice Clark clearly stated in his opinion in this case, the trial judge has the authority to order all officers of the court—which includes all lawyers and police—and all witnesses in the case to refrain from talking to news media representatives. Failure to obey such an order is contempt of court punishable by a jail sentence. In addition the trial judge has control over the conduct of everyone in the courtroom including representatives of the news media. The trial judge can even admonish the news media regarding the publication of prejudicial stories. In the Sheppard case Judge Blythin failed to make effective use of any of these powers.

The case of Sam Sheppard is not of particular significance simply because the United States Supreme Court found that Dr. Sam had not been provided his constitutional right to a fair trial. The body of decisions by the United States Supreme Court contains many cases in which the Court found that the defendant had not received a fair trial. There are, however, two significant elements in this case and Justice Clark's opinion. First, there is the evidence offered in the Court's opinion of news media influence on the judicial process through the media's exercise of their First Amendment rights—an influence that the Court said had the effect of denying Sam Sheppard his Sixth Amendment right to a fair trial. Here we can see that the conflict between the First and Sixth Amendments is not just an abstract legal concept. Second, in his opinion in this case Justice Clark provided a clear statement of the responsibility of trial judges in dealing with this conflict along with an enumeration of the powers and tools available to the trial judge to resolve this conflict.

CHAPTER 3

Doing It Right
The Tate-LaBianca Murders

Weekends are generally a slow time in the news reporting business. Saturday evening papers carry little news, and the bulk of the heavy Sunday papers is run off the presses early in the week. Thus when a really newsworthy event occurs, it receives extended coverage, and the murder of Sharon Tate was clearly such an event. From the standpoint of reader interest the murder of movie actress Sharon Tate presented almost all the ideal story ingredients—a famous victim, mystery, sexual innuendoes, and suggestions of the occult or bizarre (her husband was Roman Polanski of *Rosemary's Baby* fame).

When she arrived to begin regular work as a maid at the Roman Polanski Bel Air home in Southern California at about 9:00 A.M., Saturday, August 9, 1969, Winifred Chapman discovered an incredible scene of horror. She immediately called the police who arrived to discover the murders of Polanski's wife, Sharon Tate, and four other persons. The other four were Jay Sebring, a Hollywood hairdresser, coffee heiress Abigail Folger, Polanski's family friend Voityck Frykowski, and Steven Parent, a young man who had apparently been visiting a friend who worked as a caretaker for Polanski. The Tate and Sebring bodies were found hanging from a beam in the living room. They had been been stabbed repeatedly. The Folger and Frykowski bodies, both also dead from stab wounds, were found on the lawn, and Parent had been shot several times while sitting in his car in the driveway. There was a great deal of blood spattered around including the word "pig" written in blood on the front door. Except for Parent, all the bodies were less than fully clothed. Mrs. Polanski was eight months pregnant when she died.

As they began their investigation the police discovered caretaker William Garretson asleep in his cottage adjacent to the Polanski house. Although he claimed to know nothing of the crime, he was taken into custody as a suspect but later released. Director Roman Polanski, famous for his mysterious films, was reached at a cocktail party in London and told of the murders. He returned home while the police continued an apparently fruitless search for meaningful clues. Similar murders of Leon LaBianca and his wife a few miles away a day later were thought not to be related to the original crime. In the absence of any resolution of the case public imagination ran wild with speculation about witchcraft, drug and sex orgies, and the like. In this ambiguous situation every new speculation, each official act and comment, and any new discovery received extensive new coverage. Interviews were published, and reported efforts to solve the crime even included the use of a clairvoyant. For almost four months hardly a week went by without some report on the Tate murders.

The lead that actually began the discovery of information sufficient for indictments came by chance. In mid-October several people living in the desert east of Los Angeles were arrested on auto theft charges. Among them was Susan Atkins, who was wanted by the Los Angeles police in connection with the murder of a musician in Malibu a month prior to the Tate murders. After her transfer to a Los Angeles jail, Miss Atkins apparently made comments about other murders to her cellmate, and the cellmate reported these comments to the police. The investigation based on this new information resulted in the issuance of three indictments on December 1 that began a new round of extended public disclosures regarding the crime. Named in the indictments were Charles Watson, Patricia Kernwinkel, and Linda Kasabian, who were arrested in Texas, Alabama, and New Hampshire respectively thereby assuring further nationwide coverage of the case.

Within a day the three indicted suspects and Susan Atkins were identified as members of a hippie-style band led by Charles Manson, who at that time was in jail in a small town about fifty miles from Los Angeles on charges of suspicion of arson and receiving stolen property. The lawyer for Susan Atkins volunteered the information to the press that his client had been at the scene of both the Tate and the LaBianca murders but was under Manson's "hypnotic spell" and had nothing to do with the murders. Reporters also got a brief description of the Tate killings that was not attributed but might fairly be assumed to have come from police sources. This description included details regarding the number and sex of the murderers and the general process by which the murders were committed including the fact that Sharon Tate had pleaded, "Let me have my baby," just before she was stabbed.

On December 5, the Los Angeles County Grand Jury met to hear evidence and prepare full indictments for all those involved. While waiting for the grand jury's formal report and the inevitable leaks of the "secret" testimony before the grand jury, investigative reporting developed other information. One fairly restrained example of this reporting is the story that appeared in *The New York Times* for Sunday, December 7, 1969. This article that covered six columns on an inside page described the life of Charles Manson in some detail from his birth in 1934 to the arrest for the Tate killings. A major feature of this biography was the review of Manson's prior record of arrests and convictions although such publication was directly contrary to recommendations of the American Bar Association made in 1966 in part as a reaction to the *Sheppard* case. Among these recommendations the Bar Association's Advisory Committee on Free Press/Fair Trial concluded that publication of a prior criminal record was prejudicial to a defendant.

A week after the first break in the Tate case almost all the story became public knowledge. On December 8, the grand jury handed up a series of indictments. Manson, Susan Atkins, Linda Kasabian, Patricia Kernwinkel, and Charles Watson were all charged with the five Tate murders and the two LaBianca murders. In addition, Leslie Sankston was indicted in the LaBianca case. The publicly disclosed evidence on which the indictments were based was in large part the testimony of Susan Atkins, who gave a fully detailed confession to the crimes in an apparent effort to establish, according to her lawyer, her "diminished responsibility" because of Manson's influence. In any event the public now had a confession of the crime in some detail by one of those accused in the case.

Two days later, in the midst of frantic efforts by newsmen to feed worldwide demands for further information about the case, Los Angeles Superior Court Judge William B. Keene ordered all lawyers, public officials, police, prospective witnesses, and grand jurors not to make "any purported extra-judicial statement" about the case. This rule followed one of Justice Tom Clark's suggestions in the *Sheppard* case opinion, prohibited discussion of the case outside of court by anyone, and would, if obeyed, prevent further public statements by police, prosecutors, and Susan Atkins' lawyer. The pressure generated by newsmen's interest in the case was briefly described in a story in *The New York Times* for December 11, 1969.

> The circus aura surrounding the case was illustrated today when three of the six defendants appeared before Judge Keene to waive arraignment pending appearances later this month to enter their pleas.
>
> Dozens of newsmen crowded the courtroom and some stood on chairs to get a better look. When the lawyers entered the corridor outside the courtroom, high-intensity lights were snapped on and microphones and cameras were

poked in their faces. Several of the lawyers, while heeding Judge Keene's warning, seemed in no hurry to brush past the cameras.

On newsstands outside the Hall of Justice newspapers carried large headlines reading "New Weird Cult" and "Did Hate Kill Tate?"

While the order by Judge Keene prohibited those involved in the case from being news sources, it did not prohibit independent investigative reporting—an activity in which many eagerly engaged. One example of the results of such activity was the twelve-page lead picture article in the December 19, 1969, issue of *Life* magazine. Entitled "The Wreck of a Monstrous 'Family'," the article contained both a biography of Manson complete with interviews with two doctors and a description with pictures of the life of the Manson "family." Again Manson's prior criminal record was discussed at length.

The ultimate act in the exploitation of the public's morbid interest in the Tate-LaBianca murders came just before Christmas. Through her lawyers Susan Atkins arranged a tape recorded interview with a journalist named Lawrence Schiller. For a fee of about $80,000 to be placed in a trust fund for her infant son, Miss Atkins agreed to provide a complete first-hand account of the crimes. Police officials apparently cooperated by allowing her to leave her jail cell for the interview and thus joined Miss Atkins and her lawyer in seeming violation of Judge Keene's order. A wholly unrealistic attempt was made to limit the effect on the case of the story that was written from the interview. The story was to be sold only to European publications with the pretense that this limited sale would not result in publication in the United States even though some of the European publications were affiliated or had working agreements with publications in this country. However, even the pretended limitation became a moot point when a copy of the story was leaked to the *Los Angeles Times*, the most important newspaper in the area where the crimes were committed and the eventual trial would be held. The *Times* provided a good example of "responsible" journalism by promptly copyrighting and publishing the story. Even publications that would not stoop to printing the Atkins story found no ethical problem in reporting what less ethical publications were printing. Through the *Los Angeles Times* newswire service and European sources the story became generally available and appeared in many publications. The story eventually received full treatment in the form of a widely distributed paperback book. Schiller and those who assisted him to get the story are thought to have shared a profit of some $100,000 for their efforts.

As a result of the efforts by the press to cater to public curiosity about the Tate-LaBianca murders, the situation prior to the beginning of the trial of the defendants and the selection of an impartial jury to hear the case was as follows: The scene and victims of the murders, particularly the Tate murders, had been described in some detail and had been the subject of extensive speculation. A seemingly "official" description of the murder events had been leaked and widely published. Fairly detailed biographies of all the accused had been widely published. In particular, Charles Manson's life was examined in great detail with a great deal of attention to his past criminal record and speculation about his psychological state. Finally, a detailed firsthand account of the crimes, an apparent full confession, was provided for financial gain and given the widest possible distribution and coverage. This situation existed in spite of a judge's clear court order prohibiting all public discussion of the case by those involved as well as the existence of post-*Sheppard* press guidelines developed by the American Bar Association. These guidelines stated that is was improper to publish stories discussing a defendant's possible confession, any tests (lie detector or others) involved, past criminal record or character of the defendant, the credibility of witnesses, or anything else that might inflame public opinion against the defendant.

When the case finally came to trial in June 1970, there was a change in the list of defendants. Even though she had apparently cooperated with the grand jury, Susan Atkins remained among those charged. On the other hand the charges against Linda Kasabian were dismissed, and she became the star witness for the state. Several efforts were made to obtain a trial free of bias. Defense attorneys requested a change in venue, but this request was denied. The judge defended his ruling by pointing out that pretrial publicity had been so extensive that there was no place in California that would be free of influence from this publicity. Furthermore, the pool of potential jurors was larger in Los Angeles County than any place else in the state. Thus nothing would be gained by changing the site of the trial.

The major effort to secure a fair trial hinged on jury selection and treatment. An extensive effort was made to find jurors who would be open-minded in spite of the great amount of information they had received about the case. The process of jury selection, the voir dire examination of prospective jurors, began June 15. The selection was completed and the jury sworn on July 14. The process had taken a month.

Immediately after their selection the jury was sequestered. As a result the members of the jury were shielded from the extensive procedural arguments in court that might have influenced their attitudes toward the defendants as well as the extensive extrajudicial discussion of the case by the participants in the trial. This discussion and the wide coverage of the trial continued to reinforce the public views of the predetermined guilt of the defendants.

An example of the kind of publicity that continued during the trial and from which the jury was supposed to be shielded was the case of prospective prosecution witness Virginia Graham.

Miss Graham had shared a cell with Susan Atkins and was prepared to testify that Miss Atkins had said that the Manson group had planned to murder other celebrities including Frank Sinatra, Elizabeth Taylor, and Tom Jones. While Miss Graham's testimony was never presented in court, all the lawyers did receive transcripts of her intended testimony. The transcripts provided a basis for objections which the court sustained. The trial judge, Charles Older, ordered all attorneys not to reveal the contents of the transcript to the press. However, the full story of the testimony promptly appeared in the Los Angeles *Herald-Examiner,* whose reporter had secured copies of the transcript from unidentified members of the team of defense attorneys. Judge Older questioned all the defense attorneys, and all denied being the source of the story. The judge also questioned *Herald-Examiner* reporter William Farr, who declined to reveal the source of his story (the issue of protection of sources in this instance is discussed in full in the Appendix).

The prevailing public attitude about the case that Judge Older attempted to keep from the jury is well illustrated by a statement on law and order made by President Richard Nixon in Denver, Colorado, on August 3. Nixon, who was returning to Washington after a two-week stay at the western White House in southern California, observed that Manson was "guilty, directly or indirectly, of eight murders without reason." While this conclusion would seem reasonable on the basis of the public information about the case, the statement was newsworthy because of the source. Certainly Nixon as a lawyer and member of the California bar as well as president of the United States should have been keenly aware of the impropriety of this remark.

The next morning the *Los Angeles Times* featured a large-type banner headline that said, "MANSON GUILTY NIXON DECLARES." Extra precautions were taken to shield the jury from this news including painting over the windows of the bus that carried the jury from their hotel to the court house. These efforts were thwarted by the defendant Manson himself who somehow brought a copy of the paper into court and showed the headline to the jury. This act is but one example of the repeated disruptions by the defendants that marked this seven-month trial. The trial concluded on January 26, 1971, when, after seven days' deliberations, the jury found Manson and the other defendants guilty as charged.

Following the conviction of Manson and his followers, news coverage declined markedly. Although legal action continued and other trials on other charges were begun, the Manson group no longer provided regular nightly segments for the network television news. Whether because there was no more suspense, because curiosity had been satisfied, or because the public's short attention span had been exhausted, the Manson clan was no longer newsworthy. However, attempts at commercial exploitation continued. Several jurors indicated their intention to publish accounts of the trial and the life of the sequestered jury during the seven months of the trial. In 1974 the chief prosecutor at the trial, Vincent Bugliosi, did publish his account of the case. Rather than focus on the sensational elements of the case, the book detailed the problems of developing and presenting the case at trial and included specifics of the many errors made by the police in the course of the investigation of the crimes. Bugliosi's book was later made into the movie *Helter Skelter*.

The handling of the Tate-LaBianca murder trial is in sharp contrast to the handling of the Sheppard trial. The problems were significantly greater because of the greater public interest due in large part due to the fame of the movie star victim and her friends and husband. All the judges involved in the case demonstrated a keen awareness of the problem and took the steps available to them as outlined by Justice Clark in the *Sheppard* case opinion to assure the Manson group a fair trial. When the defendants were indicted, Judge Keene directed that all the officers of the court—all lawyers, witnesses, and police—should not make any statements about the case to the news media. Clearly some of these officers of the court, for money or other reasons, anonymously violated Judge Keene's and later Judge Older's orders.

Judge Older rejected the defense request for a change of venue on reasonable grounds. The crime was a violation of California law and had to be tried in that state. The publicity about the case was no doubt seen and heard everywhere. Thus Los Angeles County with the largest pool of jurors from which to choose was the logical place for the trial. Extensive voir dire examination resulted in the selection of an impartial jury which was then sequestered to guarantee that the members would not be influenced by anything other than the trial testimony. In a final bizarre twist in this bizarre case the principal defendant teamed with the president of the United States (as a member of the California bar, also an officer of the court) to create the only significant breach of this tight security.

The judges involved with the Tate-LaBianca murders trial used the power available to them to protect the defendants' Sixth Amendment right to a fair trial without violating the First Amendment rights of the news media. These efforts were only partially successful due to: 1) extreme public curiosity about the case, 2) news media efforts to satisfy public curiosity, 3) those seeking financial gain from the case, 4) the self-destructive actions of the defendants and their lawyers, and 5) irresponsible comments by a high public official carelessly permitted entry into the courtroom.

CHAPTER 4

An Attempt to Make the Media Live by Their Own Rules
The Kellie Family Murders

S ome time after 9:00 P.M. Saturday, October 18, 1975, police were called to the home of Henry Kellie in Sutherland, Nebraska. There they found the bodies of sixty-six-year-old Kellie, his fifty-seven-year-old wife Marie, his son David (thirty-two), and three grandchildren: Florence (eleven), Deanne (six), and Daniel (five). All had been killed by shotgun blasts—Kellie had been shot three times. Word of the crime was received by the news media, and a local radio station broadcast a police bulletin that an armed sniper was in the area. Everyone was advised to stay indoors, keep their doors locked, and refuse to open them to strangers. The citizens of Sutherland, population 840, spent a very anxious night.

By Sunday morning, news of this shocking crime had spread throughout the community. The magnitude of the event for Sutherland can be seen by the fact that a murder in the city of Chicago with an equivalent proportion of victims would involve 21,000 deaths. Acting on a tip, police found Erwin Charles Simants, age thirty, hiding in the woods behind his parents' house where he lived. The house was next door to the Kellie residence. Simants was arraigned in Lincoln County Court later that same day.

On Monday, October 20, the story of the murders and Simants' arrest for the crimes dominated the news on radio, television, and the newspapers. Reporters discovered that Simants had apparently admitted the murders to his parents, who called the police. In addition it was revealed that Simants had also given the police a confession. Speculation regarding the motive for the crime and the mental state of the accused was widespread. Autopsies later confirmed the truth of the rumor that Simants had raped both Mrs. Kellie and her granddaughter, Florence, after he had killed them.

Tuesday afternoon October 21, Simants court appointed lawyer and the Lincoln County attorney appeared before County Judge Ronald Ruff to discuss the problem of providing Simants with a fair trial in light of the widespread and extensive reporting about the crime. This hearing took place in county seat of North Platte whose population of 19,000 was two-thirds of the total county population. Nebraska state law severely restricted two of the usual techniques used to assure fair trial—continuance and change of venue. The statutes required that the accused must be brought to trial within six months. In addition, any change of venue could only move the trial to an adjoining county, every one of which was less populous than Lincoln County. The city of North Platte, just twenty miles east of Sutherland, was clearly the urban center for this entire area of southwest Nebraska. The county attorney presented the following motion:

> The State of Nebraska hereby represented unto the court that by reason of the nature of the above-captioned [Simants] case, there has been, and no doubt there will continue to be, mass coverage by news media not only locally but nationally as well; that a preliminary hearing on the charges has been set to commence at 9:00 A.M. on October 22, 1975; and that there is a reasonable likelihood of prejudicial news which would make difficult, if not impossible, the impaneling of an impartial jury and tend to prevent a

fair trial should the defendant be bound over to trial in the District Court if testimony of witnesses at the preliminary hearing is reported to the public.

Therefore the State of Nebraska moves that the Court forthwith enter a Restrictive Order setting forth the matter that may or may not be publicly reported or disclosed to the public with reference to said case or with reference to the preliminary hearing thereon, and to whom said order shall apply.

No evidence beyond the claims made in the state's petition was presented.

The following morning at the preliminary hearing Judge Ruff issued a restrictive order. All lawyers, court personnel, witnesses, police, "and any other person present in Court" were directed not to "release for public dissemination in any form or manner whatsoever any testimony given or evidence adduced during the preliminary hearing." In addition any information disseminated was to conform with the "Nebraska Bar-Press Guidelines for Disclosure and Reporting of Information Relating to Imminent or Pending Criminal Litigation." These voluntary guidelines had been drawn up in 1970 to provide suggestions of what the press should do to avoid interfering with a defendant's Sixth Amendment rights. The guidelines were closely related to the British standards in that they provided for the publication only of the basic facts of the crime and arrest. The list of inappropriate subjects included confessions (if any), opinions about guilt or trial outcome, and the results of any kinds of tests (or the failure to take them). News media were admonished to exercise special caution about publishing any prior criminal record of the accused. With these restrictions in place the preliminary hearing was held, and Simants was bound over to trial.

The effect of Judge Ruff's order was clear. The news media were prohibited from publishing most of what had taken place at

the preliminary hearing as well as other information about the
case that had not been clearly specified. Media representatives
considered the order to be a clear violation of the freedom of
speech and press guaranteed by the First Amendment. The following day, Thursday October 23, a petition was filed with the
district court asking that the county court order be vacated. The
petition was received by the district court judge, Hugh Stuart
who then held a hearing at which Judge Ruff explained the reasons for his order. No other testimony was presented, and Judge
Stuart allowed the restrictive order to remain in effect until he
had time to rule on the petition. On Monday October 27, Judge
Stuart terminated the county court order and replaced it with one
of his own. The judge found that "because of the nature of the
crimes charged in the complaint . . . there is a clear and present
danger that pre-trial publicity could impinge upon the defendant's
right to a fair trial and that an order setting forth the limitation
of *pre-trial* publicity [emphasis added] is appropriate." The specific terms of Judge Stuart's order were as follows:

> 1. It is hereby stated the trial of the case commences
> when a jury is empaneled to try the case, and that all re-
> porting prior to that event, specifically including the pre-
> liminary hearing, is "pre-trial" publicity.
> 2. It would appear that the defendant has made a state-
> ment or confession to law enforcement officials and it is
> inappropriate to report the existence of such statement or
> the contents of it.
> 3. It appears that the defendant may have made state-
> ments against interest to James Robert Boggs, Amos Si-
> mants and Grace Simants, and may have left a note in the
> William Boggs residence, and that the nature of such state-
> ments, or the fact that such statements were made, or the
> nature of the testimony of these witnesses with reference to

such statements in the preliminary hearing will not be reported.

4. The non-technical aspects of the testimony of Dr. Miles Foster [the coroner] may be reported within the [bar-press] guidelines and at the careful discretion of the press. The testimony of this witness dealing with technical subjects, tests or investigations performed or the results thereof, or his opinions and conclusions as a result of such tests or investigations will not be reported.

5. The general physical facts found at the scene of the crime may be reported within the guidelines and at the careful discretion of the press. However, the identity of the person or persons allegedly sexually assaulted or the details of any alleged assault by the defendant will not be reported.

6. The exact nature of the limitations of publicity as entered by the order will not be reported. This is to say, the fact of the entering of this order limiting pre-trial publicity and the adoption of the Bar-Press Guidelines may be reported, but specific reference to confessions, statements against interest, witnesses or type of evidence to which this order will apply will not be reported.

Even though Judge Stuart's order was carefully drawn to deal with only the most sensitive elements of pretrial publicity and would automatically dissolve once Simants' trial began, the news media were naturally dissatisfied. The order was still seen as a prior restraint in violation of the First Amendment. Media representatives appealed to both the Nebraska Supreme Court and United States Supreme Court Justice Harry Blackmun, as circuit judge for Nebraska, asking that the order be lifted. Justice Blackmun declined to consider the issue until after the Nebraska court had acted. The Nebraska Supreme Court then considered the matter and finally on December 1, issued an opinion that in large part upheld the court order as Judge Stuart had issued it. Media representatives then petitioned the entire United States Supreme Court to accept the case, and the Court agreed.

In the meantime preparations went forward for the speedy trial of Erwin Simants, and proceedings began on Monday, January 5, 1976. Preliminary motions and jury selection took three days. Not surprisingly, every prospective juror from Sutherland was excused in the course of the voir dire examination. On Thursday, January 8, the jury was sworn and sequestered, Judge Stuart's restrictive order terminated, and Erwin Simants' murder trial began. The prosecution case with witnesses and confession testimony was presented essentially as outlined at the preliminary hearing eleven weeks earlier. The case for the defense rested on the grounds that Simants was insane as well as an alcoholic who was drunk at the time of the murders and sexual assaults. After a seven-day trial the case went to the jury on Friday, January 16, and after four and one-half hours of deliberation the jury found Simants guilty on all charges.

Even though the Kellie murder case was closed, the controversy over Judge Stuart's order continued. The case was argued before the United States Supreme Court on April 19, 1976. On one side were lawyers for the State of Nebraska representing Judge Stuart. The state's position was that Judge Stuart's order was a carefully drawn and limited order designed to respond to the "clear and present danger" to Erwin Simants' Sixth Amendment right to a fair trial. Furthermore, the order was nothing more than a judicial recognition of standards of conduct to which the media had already voluntarily agreed.

Lawyers on the other side represented the Nebraska Press Association and the National Broadcasting Company and were supported by written briefs filed by the American Civil Liberties Union, the American Newspaper Publishers Association, the National Press Club, and a number of other individuals and groups. The basic position of all these groups was that Judge Stuart' order was an unconstitutional violation of the First Amendment's guarantee of freedom of speech and press. The order prohibiting publication of information was what is called a prior restraint, and in previous cases of this type the United States Supreme Court had always found such rules unconstitutional.

The Supreme Court handed down its decision on June 30. While the justices unanimously found that Judge Stuart's order had been a violation of the First Amendment, they were unable to arrive at any clear consensus about the reasons for this conclusion. The nine justices wrote five separate opinions none of which was supported by more than four justices. Through a careful examination of these opinions it is possible to extract some general principles from the muddle.

First, the justices all seemed to agree that this prior restraint violated the First Amendment. In all the previous Supreme Court cases that dealt with prior restraint the Court has suggested only the most limited exception to the general rule that such restraints are unconstitutional. For example, publication of the location of troopships at sea in wartime might be constitutionally prohibited. However, in this case the justices were unwilling to create a new category of permissible restraint.

Second, all the justices seemed to recognize Judge Stuart's problem in attempting to secure a fair trial for Erwin Simants. They agree that he acted responsibly in attempting to deal with these problems. In fact many pages of the opinions review the actual circumstances of the crime, arrest, and trial. The pervasiveness of information about the case in such sparsely populated places as Sutherland and Lincoln County was duly noted along with the nature and magnitude of the crime that would assure great public interest and attention. It was further noted that these very circumstances probably made the restrictive orders ineffective since the information being withheld was widely circulated by word of mouth along with rumors and conjecture that might have been more harmful to the defendant than accurate facts.

Justice William Brennan noted that every prospective juror from Sutherland was dismissed during voir dire.

Third, there was apparent agreement that in spite of all the pretrial publicity problems, the techniques to assure fair trial reviewed by Justice Tom Clark in the *Sheppard* case would have been sufficient to assure Simants' Sixth Amendment rights. In previous cases the Supreme Court had ruled that state law cannot constitutionally limit the use of the techniques of continuance and change of venue when the defendant requests these remedies. Prohibiting statements to the news media by all officers of the court and witnesses is also appropriate. It was noted that the orders by both Judge Rupp and Judge Stuart made use of this remedy. The use of careful voir dire examination of prospective jurors and sequestering the jury were also warmly supported by the justices and were in fact used in this case.

Finally, an interesting suggestion emerged in the footnotes to the two longest opinions. Chief Justice Warren Burger noted that a number of studies have suggested that it might be appropriate to close pretrial proceedings when this remedy is requested by the defendant, and Justice William Brennan observed that Nebraska law did not require that preliminary hearings be open to the public. He added that "the question whether preliminary hearings may be closed to the public consistently with the 'Public Trial' Clause of the Sixth Amendment is not before us, and it is therefore one on which I would express no view."

In summary, the Supreme Court concluded that while pretrial publicity such as that to which Erwin Simants was subjected might inhibit a defendant's ability to receive a fair trial, prohibiting the news media from publishing information available to them is not constitutionally permissible. Trial courts can, however, inhibit the flow of information to the media through valid orders restraining the actions of those involved in the case and trial. There is even the suggestion that pretrial proceedings might be closed to the public to protect the defendant's Sixth Amendment rights. Furthermore, a variety of techniques—continuance, change of venue, voir dire, sequestering—can be used to assure, as far as possible, that the defendant's case is presented to an impartial jury.

CHAPTER 5

The Closed Pretrial Evidentiary Hearing

The Missing Wayne Clapp

Wayne Clapp, a forty-two year old former town policeman, lived in the Rochester, New York, suburb of Henrietta. He also owned a cottage on Seneca Lake about forty miles from Rochester where he kept a boat that he used for his favorite sport of fishing. He was last seen on Friday, July 16, 1976, when he left shore in his boat to go fishing with two male companions, one of whom was known to those who witnessed the departure as Kyle E. Greathouse, age sixteen. Later in the day Greathouse and the other man returned alone, tied up the boat, and drove away in Clapp's pickup truck.

The following Monday when Clapp failed to return from his weekend fishing trip, his family notified the police that he was missing. Seneca County officers went to his cottage where they found Clapp's boat with several bullet holes in it. The combination of the missing man, the bullet holes, and the missing pickup truck led police to suspect that a crime had been committed. They began dragging the lake to find Clapp's body. Further investigation revealed that Greathouse and his wife Marilea (also age sixteen) were missing from the room that they were renting at Mauro's Lakeview Inn on Seneca Lake as was their friend David R. Jones, who was twenty-one. Police issued arrest warrants and a bulletin describing the three suspects and Clapp's missing truck. The next day, Tuesday July 22, the Rochester daily newspapers both carried stories about Clapp's disappearance including the facts known at that time, the investigative activities of the police, and the names and descriptions of the suspects in the case.

Wednesday morning, police in Jackson County, Michigan, discovered Clapp's pickup truck parked at a local motel. The investigating officers found Jones in a park nearby and arrested him. They then began a search for the Greathouses who had fled into the adjacent woods. With the aid of a helicopter and dogs the two were tracked down and arrested. Stories about the capture of the three appeared in Thursday's Rochester newspapers. In addition to recounting the details of the arrests, these stories reported speculation by Seneca County police that Clapp had been shot with his own gun, robbed, and his body then thrown into Seneca Lake, the largest and deepest (600 feet) of all the Finger Lakes, where it might never be found. It was also reported that the Seneca County district attorney intended to press murder charges even if the body was never recovered.

After their capture, Jones and the Greathouses apparently decided that further efforts to avoid punishment were futile. Kyle Greathouse led police to the place where Clapp's .357 magnum pistol had been buried. Police found ammunition at the motel where the suspects had stayed prior to their arrest. All three waived extradition and were returned to Seneca County Saturday July 24, where they were formally charged with the murder of Wayne Clapp. At that arraignment hearing sworn statements by three witnesses that they had heard shots the day Clapp disappeared and had seen his boat "veer sharply" in the water were introduced as evidence against the accused. All this information as well as some personal background about the accused, appeared in stories in the Rochester newspapers Friday, Saturday, and Sunday, July 23, 24, and 25.

Ten days later, Monday August 2, a Seneca County grand jury handed up indictments. Jones and Kyle Greathouse were charged with second-degree murder, robbery, and grand larceny. Marilea Greathouse was charged only with grand larceny. The indictments charged that the two men shot Wayne Clapp with his own gun, weighted the body with the boat anchors, and threw it in the lake. They took Clapp's gun, credit cards, and truck and fled to Michigan. That same evening a memorial service was held for Clapp, whose body had not been recovered, in his home town of Henrietta. On Thursday August 4, the three suspects were formally arraigned on the grand jury indictments, and all three pleaded not guilty to all of the charges. Once again news stories in the Rochester papers of August 3 and 6 reported these events.

Under New York state law those accused of crimes have a ninety-day period after their formal arraignment to file pretrial motions. During this period lawyers for the accused presented motions asking that evidence against the accused be suppressed. The Fifth Amendment to the Constitution states that an accused person cannot be forced to testify against himself. This guarantee means that a suspect cannot be tortured to secure evidence. The courts have also ruled that a suspect cannot be tricked in any way and must be informed of the right to remain silent. Any statement made to police must be entirely voluntary and based on a clear understanding by the suspect of the right to remain silent. In this case the lawyers argued that the accused had not been informed of their rights at the time that they made statements to the Michigan police. In addition, the physical evidence gained as a result of these statements—Clapp's pistol and the ammunition for it—should also not be allowed as trial evidence.

A hearing on these pretrial motions was held before Seneca County Court Judge Daniel DePasquale on Thursday November , at the end of the ninety-day filing period. Because the police had little evidence other than the incriminating statements made by the accused and the pistol found as a result of these statements, the action by the court on the motions to suppress was important to both sides. The basic rule of law here is that evidence that has

been improperly obtained cannot be used as trial evidence. Thi
rule, called the Exclusionary Rule, might seem to be unfair be
cause a guilty person could go free because clear evidence of guil
was not allowed to be presented. However, over the years th
courts have determined that the best protection against imprope
police conduct is to exclude the results of that illegal activit
from use as trial evidence. If police could use a confession ob
tained by beating a suspect, the Fifth Amendment guarante
against self-incrimination would mean nothing. If police coul
use physical evidence however obtained, the right to be protecte
against unlawful search provided in the Fourth Amendment woul
also be meaningless. Without the Exclusionary Rule the integrit
of the judicial process could be called into question and publi
confidence in our system of justice undermined. Unfortunatel
violations of constitutional rights do occur, and violations ma
have taken place in this case.

At the start of the hearing the lawyers for Jones and the Greatl
ouses asked that the hearing be closed to the public and the pres
They claimed that there had been excessive and adverse publicit
concerning the case and pointed out that suppression of admi
sions and physical evidence would have little value if these admi
sions and the evidence suppressed were reported to prospecti
jurors through the press. The prosecuting attorney indicated th
he had no objection. Thereupon Judge DePasquale agreed to clo
the hearing and ordered those present, including newspaper r
porter Carol Ritter, to leave the courtroom. All did as directe
without objection, and the hearing was closed.

The next morning Ritter handed Judge DePasquale a lett
prepared with the help of the lawyers working for the Ganne
Company, the owner of the two Rochester daily newspapers.
the letter the reporter claimed the "right to cover this hearin
and requested that "we . . . be given access to the transcript"
the closed hearing of the day before. Judge DePasquale answer
that the suppression hearing had been completed. He added th

he would take under consideration the request for the transcript. The Gannett Company then asked the New York State Supreme Court (the name given to the original trial courts in this state's court system) to set aside Judge DePasquale's order. It might be noted here that the Gannett Company has not always been a defender of the constitutional right of public access to judicial proceedings. In 1975 in Salem, Oregon, Gannett was sued by a competitor that claimed it had been driven out of business by Gannett's illegal practices. Gannett settled the suit out of court and then successfully petitioned the court to seal the pretrial records so that the press would be unable to inform the public of the details of Garnett's alleged misconduct.

At this point two separate legal processes were under way. In the first the case against Jones and the Greathouses moved toward trial in Seneca County. In the second the state supreme court in Rochester held a hearing on Tuesday, November 16, on the Gannett request to vacate Judge DePasquale's order. On the basis of this hearing the supreme court reached the following conclusions: 1) As a general principle the press has a constitutional right of access to court proceedings. 2) Objection to Judge DePasquale's order should have been made by those present at the time the order was issued. 3) The trial judge has a responsibility to balance the public's right of access to court proceedings against the right of a defendant to a fair trial. In this case Judge DePasquale was correct in finding that to open the suppression hearing to the public would create a "reasonable probability of prejudice to these defendants." Thus, the supreme court refused to vacate Judge DePasquale's order or to grant public access to the hearing transcript.

The next day this ruling was appealed to the next level of New York state courts, the appellate division of the supreme court, which also held court in Rochester. This court conducted a full-scale hearing on the issue at which the Gannett lawyers presented a number of constitutional arguments. They claimed that the closure of the hearing violated the First Amendment guarantee of freedom of the press because the newspapers were unable to report what had happened. They pointed out that the Sixth Amendment states specifically that "the accused shall enjoy the right to a speedy and *public* [emphasis added] trial." Finally they noted that the Fourteenth Amendment requires that all states must grant to defendants "due process of law," part of which is a public trial.

While the appellate division was considering its ruling on the Gannett motion, back in Seneca County the Jones and Greathouse case moved forward. As a result of Judge DePasquale's denial of the request to suppress evidence, lawyers for the defendants entered into discussions with the prosecutor designed to settle the case. This process, sometimes called plea bargaining, is common in the criminal judicial system. In New York State more than ninety percent of all criminal cases never come to trial because the defendants plead guilty as charged, guilty to some lesser charge, or the charges are dismissed. In the second case the prosecution agrees to accept a guilty plea to the lesser charge in full satisfaction of all the charges against the defendant. The trial court judge plays a role in this process in that the judge must decide to accept the agreement worked out by the prosecutor and the defense lawyers. In Seneca County in 1976, through the use of these procedures, not a single criminal case came to trial. Jones and the Greathouses avoided trial on the murder charges by pleading guilty to the grand larceny and robbery charges. This bargain would seem to have been a good one for both prosecution and defense. On the one hand the guilt of the defendants seemed clear. On the other it might be difficult to get a jury to convict the defendants of murder without the body of the victim. In addition an appeals court might reverse Judge DePasquale and rule that the admissions to the Michigan police and the gun could not be used as evidence. Judge DePasquale accepted these guilty pleas, sentenced the defendants to jail, and released the transcript of the closed pretrial suppression hearing.

While the situation created by Judge DePasquale's action had now been resolved in fact, the legal issues remained unsettled. On December 17, 1976, the Appellate Division of the New York State Supreme Court, Fourth Department, issued a ruling stating that Judge DePasquale had violated the public's interest in open judicial proceedings. In addition, the court agreed with the Gannett lawyers that the order also violated both the First and Fourteenth Amendments. Seneca County lawyers representing Judge DePasquale appealed this decision to New York's highest state court, the Court of Appeals. Shortly after the first of the year, the Court of Appeals reversed the appellate division and decided the case in favor of Judge DePasquale. In this ruling the Court of Appeals pointed to the widespread publicity that the case had received, which included information that the defendants "had been caught 'red-handed' by Michigan police with the fruits of the crime" and "had made incriminating statements before being returned to" New York. The decision went on to say:

> Widespread public awareness kindled by media saturation does not legitimize mere curiosity. Here the public's concern was not focused on prosecutorial or judicial accountability; irregularities, if any, had occurred out of state. The interest of the public was chiefly one of active curiosity with respect to a notorious local happening.

The court balanced the right of the defendants to a fair trial by an impartial jury against this public curiosity and concluded that Judge DePasquale had acted properly to protect the defendants' rights.

Although New York State's highest court had ruled that Judge DePasquale had acted properly, and James Jones and William and

Nancy Greathouse had been sentenced and sent to jail, the case was still not over. The Gannett Company asked the United States Supreme Court to consider the constitutional issues raised by Judge DePasquale's order. That court agreed to hear the case. Oral arguments were presented on November 7, 1978, and the Gannett Company position was supported by an array of written arguments offered by a number of interested groups including the American Civil Liberties Union, the American Newspaper Publishers Association, Sigma Delta Chi, the Reporters Committee for Freedom of the Press, and the New York Times Company. On July 2, 1979, almost three years after Wayne Clapp departed on that fateful fishing trip, the Supreme Court issued its decision and opinions which finally concluded the case.

By a vote of five to four the Supreme Court decided that Judge DePasquale's action in closing a pretrial hearing was constitutional and proper. The majority's reasoning behind its decision as expressed in four separate opinions was once again unclear. The basic position taken by the majority was that the right of a public trial belonged to the accused as clearly stated in the words of the Sixth Amendment. The majority rejected the position taken by the four minority justices that the public at large also had a meaningful interest in open and public judicial proceedings.

The extent of the accused's right to secrecy was unclear in Justice Potter Stewart's opinion for the Court majority. In his review of the history of open judicial proceedings and the limited exceptions to that general principle, Justice Stewart suggested that different standards might apply to actual trials than might apply to pretrial suppression hearings. However, in a dozen places in the opinion Stewart seemed to say that the Court's decision on pretrial hearings also applied to trials. The confusion was increased by the opinions of the concurring justices. Chief Justice Warren Burger stated explicitly, "By definition a hearing on motion before trial to suppress evidence is not a *trial*; it is *pre*trial hearing [emphasis in the original]." On the other hand

Justice William Rhenquist, consistent with his demonstrated long-standing hostility toward freedom of speech and press, stated his understanding of the Court's decision as follows:

> The Court today holds, without qualification, that "members of the public have no constitutional right under the Sixth and Fourteenth Amendments to attend criminal trials." . . . [S]ince the court holds that the public does not have *any* Sixth Amendment right of access to such proceedings, it necessarily follows that if the parties agree on a closed proceeding, the trial court is not required by the Sixth Amendment to advance any reason whatsoever for declining to open a pretrial hearing or trial to the public [emphasis in the original].

And Justice Lewis Powell, another member of the Court majority in this case, disagreed with this position. In his concurring opinion Powell described the extent of danger to a fair trial that would need to be shown before a defendant's motion to close a pretrial hearing could be properly accepted. He observed that he felt the facts of the Jones and Greathouse case satisfied these requirements.

The single opinion for the four-justice minority, written by Justice Harry Blackmun, was clear and unequivocal. The minority rejected the contention that there had been excessive publicity in this case that would make the selection of an impartial jury difficult. Blackmun also provided a detailed historical review of the concept of a public trial from Anglo-Saxon criminal proceedings before the Norman conquest (pre-1066) to current federal and state laws and rulings on the question. This review established that public trial was a central and unquestioned principle in Anglo-American jurisprudence. Furthermore, the public's interest in seeing that justice is done provided the basis for the public's Sixth Amendment interest in a public trial.

At long last Judge Daniel DePasquale's order closing a pretrial suppression hearing in his Seneca County courtroom had been upheld after review by four different higher courts. Even though the United States Supreme Court had spoken, the issues raised by this case had not been settled. The closely divided Court, the confusion in the majority position, and the detail force of the dissenting opinion all suggested that the United States Supreme Court might have to deal with the issue again some time in the future.

While this Supreme Court decision seemed to authorize the closing of pretrial hearings on the suppression of evidence, a number of lower court rulings since 1979 have had the effect of sharply limiting this judicial remedy for free press–fair trial conflicts. When such a remedy is proposed, lawyers for the accused are usually required to demonstrate that real harm will flow from an open hearing. Judges are required to balance the public's right to know against the trial rights of the accused. News organizations usually contest vigorously, including appeals to higher courts, any decision to close a pretrial hearing.

CHAPTER 6

"The Right to a Speedy and Public Trial"
Who Killed Lillian Keller?

In 1975 Howard Franklin Bittorf of Baltimore, Maryland, was separated from his wife and living in the Holly Court Motel on U.S. Route 1 just outside of Ashland about fifteen miles north of Richmond, Virginia. His motel room connected to the apartment of motel manager Lillian Keller, and during his stay at the motel, he and Mrs. Keller had established a close relationship. At the beginning of December 1975, Bittorf's brother-in-law, John Paul Stevenson, came down from Baltimore to visit him. He also developed a friendship with Mrs. Keller and spent most of the night of December 1–2 with her in her apartment. In the morning of December 2, Bittorf and Stevenson were joined by Jeffrey Taylor, who also had a room at the Holly Court Motel, and the three went out drinking. After a day of drinking vodka with beer chasers, Stevenson said that he passed out in the back seat of Bittorf's car. Bittorf reportedly returned to the Holly Court Motel to pick up clothing for a visit to Baltimore. At that time he and Taylor talked with Mrs. Keller, who was said to have told Taylor to get a job so that he could pay his rent. Taylor went to his room while Bittorf packed. When he was ready to leave, Bittorf knocked on Taylor's door. Taylor did not respond, and Bittorf left without him with Stevenson still passed out in the back seat.

At about 6:30 that evening, Lillian Keller's son, Barry Kitzin, stopped by to see his mother. He found her partially clothed and bloody body lying on the floor of her apartment bedroom and immediately called the police. The police investigation disclosed that Mrs. Keller had been beaten and died of stab wounds. The motel office had also been robbed. The investigation quickly focused on Howard Bittorf, who was gone from his adjacent room, and his companions John Paul Stevenson and Jeffrey Taylor. Taylor was questioned and the search began for Bittorf and Stevenson, who were eventually found and arrested in Wisconsin. They were returned to Virginia and charged with the murder at a preliminary hearing in Hanover County General District Court on December 19, 1975. Formal indictments were returned against the two in March 1976, and the first defendant, John Paul Stevenson, went to trial in mid-July.

The evidence presented at the Stevenson trial was of two types—physical evidence and the testimony of Bittorf, Taylor, and Stevenson. In the area of physical evidence the Commonwealth of Virginia presented a wallet found on the floor near Mrs. Keller's body. The wallet contained Stevenson's Maryland driver's license. In Bittorf's room the police had found a bloodstained knife, the apparent murder weapon, and a bloody towel. There were, however, no identifiable fingerprints. A knit pullover shirt said to belong to Stevenson was also presented. A police officer testified that he had gone to Baltimore December 5, three days after the crime, and had talked to Stevenson's wife. The officer asked if Stevenson had changed clothes when he returned to Baltimore on the second, and Mrs. Stevenson gave him the shirt that she said he had been wearing. The shirt was subjected to a laboratory examination during which a small stain was found that was determined to be human blood of a type consistent with Lillian Keller's blood. Only 4.7 percent of the population have this type blood.

The testimony of the defendant and his friends presented a

confusing picture for the jury. Stevenson's testimony was short and simple. He had been with Lillian Keller in the early morning hours of December 2 and had left her to go out drinking. He passed out in the back seat of Howard Bittorf's car, did not regain consciousness until he arrived in Baltimore, and had not seen Lillian Keller again. Howard Bittorf's testimony supported Stevenson's account of the day. He added that when they returned to the Holly Court Motel, he and Jeffrey Taylor had seen and talked with Mrs. Keller, who admonished Taylor to get a job. Taylor went to his room and did not answer Bittorf's knock when it was time to leave for Baltimore. Mrs. Keller, who Bittorf said was "just like a wife to me," was alive and well when Bittorf drove off with Stevenson still passed out in the back seat.

Jeffrey Taylor's account of the events of the afternoon of December 2, 1975, was different than that of Bittorf and Stevenson. Taylor said that when the three returned to the motel, Stevenson had also gone to Bittorf's room. At Stevenson's suggestion he and Stevenson pretended to be having a fight, which angered Mrs. Keller. When he left to go to his room, Taylor said he heard Bittorf and Mrs. Keller having a loud argument. Taylor also testified that Stevenson was wearing a long-sleeve buttoned shirt with the sleeves rolled up on the day of the crime.

In summarizing the case for the jury Stevenson's lawyer pointed the finger of guilt at Jeffrey Taylor. He claimed that the motive was money and that Taylor had "set up" Bittorf and Stevenson to shift suspicion from himself. This line of argument did not persuade the jury which, perhaps influenced more by the physical evidence, found John Paul Stevenson guilty of murder in the death of Lillian Keller. Stevenson was sentenced to ten years in prison, and his lawyer gave notice that he intended to appeal the conviction. The following week Howard Franklin Bittorf came to trial for the same crime, was found guilty, and was sentenced to twenty years in prison. At this trial Jeffrey Taylor expanded his testimony to say that Bittorf told him that he was going to steal money from the motel and had shown him the bills when he returned from Mrs. Keller's apartment.

An additional result of Jeffrey Taylor's testimony at the trials of John Paul Stevenson and Howard Franklin Bittorf was his indictment in September 1976, in connection with the death of Lillian Keller. At his trial two months later, the Commonwealth of Virginia presented physical evidence in the form of samples taken from the crime scene that were consistent with Taylor's hair and blood according to the forensic scientist who testified at the trial. The commonwealth's attorney argued that Taylor was a full participant in the plot to murder Mrs. Keller and steal her money. However, at least some of the jury were not persuaded. The jury reported that it was hopelessly deadlocked, and a mistrial was declared. Taylor fared even better when he was retried the following month. The trial judge accepted the defense motion for acquittal because of insufficient evidence. Thus, one year and eleven days after Lillian Keller was murdered two of those charged were convicted and in prison, and the third had been found not guilty.

As he had promised at the trial, John Paul Stevenson's lawyer did appeal his client's conviction. Although the two Richmond daily newspapers, the *News Leader* and the *Times-Dispatch*, had reported fully on the Keller murder, the investigation, the arrests, and the four trials of the three accused, Stevenson's appeal was not based on undue publicity. Rather, attorney C. Willard Norwood presented an argument based on the admissibility of evidence. The key piece of physical evidence to connect Stevenson to the crime was the knit shirt with the bloodstain that he was said to have been wearing on the day of the crime. However, that connection was the testimony of a police officer who reported that Mrs. Stevenson had said that the shirt had been worn by Stevenson on the day in question (Mrs. Stevenson did not testify). Jeffrey Taylor had testified that Stevenson had been wearing a different shirt. The officer's report of what someone else said is hearsay which under the standard rules of evidence is inadmissible in a criminal trial. Since there was no allowable evidence that Stevenson had been wearing this shirt on December 2, 1975, there was no legal foundation for introducing either the shirt or the tests of the bloodstain on the shirt as evidence against Stevenson. Thus on October 7, 1977, the Virginia Supreme Court reversed Stevenson's conviction and ordered that he receive a new trial in which the illegal evidence would not be presented. Attorney Norwood also secured a reversal for Howard Franklin Bittorf because the "Stevenson shirt" had been used at his trial as well.

John Paul Stevenson's second trial for the murder of Lillian Keller began in the Hanover Circuit Court of Judge Richard H. C. Taylor on May 30, 1978. A voir dire examination of prospective jurors was conducted, and a panel selected and sworn. At this point one of the selected jurors asked to be excused because she had a nervous condition for which she was taking tranquilizers. Judge Taylor excused the juror and, because there were no longer twelve jurors to hear the case, dismissed the rest of the jury and declared a mistrial. The judge also ordered that Stevenson was to go to trial again in just one week. The stories of the mistrial that appeared in the Richmond newspapers and that were broadcast included accounts of the original crime and trial as well as the evidence that the Virginia Supreme Court had found inadmissible.

As the new trial (Stevenson's third on the charge) began June 6, Stevenson's lawyer, C. Willard Norwood, asked that the trial be closed in order to protect his client's Sixth Amendment rights. Judge Taylor agreed with this request. The courtroom was closed to the public and press, and jury selection began. A little over a half hour later the courtroom doors were opened, the jury dismissed, and another mistrial declared. At the time the reason for this action was not known since Judge Taylor had ordered all those involved not to talk to the press. However, it was later revealed that the mistrial had occurred when one prospective juror who had read about Stevenson's prior trials in the newspapers began to tell the other jurors about them.

John Paul Stevenson's fourth trial for the murder of Lillian Keller began before Judge Richard Taylor on Monday, September 11, 1978. Once again attorney Norwood moved that the trial be closed, and once again Judge Taylor granted his request. As the trial continued behind closed doors, lawyers for the two Richmond daily newspapers presented a motion asking that the court be opened to the public and press. Judge Taylor agreed to hear that motion after the Stevenson trial concluded for the day but ruled that the hearing was part of the trial and would be conducted in private. The subsequent release of the hearing transcript showed that Judge Taylor agreed with the defense attorney's argument that the particular problems of four trials justified special measures to protect his client's rights. The following day the trial of John Paul Stevenson concluded, and its outcome was reported in the following court order:

> At the conclusion of the Commonwealth's evidence, the attorney for the defendant moved the Court to strike the Commonwealth's evidence on grounds stated in the record, which Motion was sustained by the Court. And the jury having been excused, the Court doth find the accused NOT GUILTY of Murder, as charged in the Indictment, and he was allowed to depart.

In plain language Judge Taylor found that the evidence presented by the prosecution was inadequate to support a guilty verdict, and he dismissed the charge. Since the case had been presented in secret, there was no way for the public to evaluate Judge Taylor's conclusion. However, the prosecutor in all four trials, Patrick R. Bynum, indicated no strong objection to the decision in an interview with reporters. Without the evidence suppressed by the Virginia Supreme Court his case was at best circumstantial.

While Stevenson's days in court were now over, for the *Richmond News Leader* and *Richmond Times-Dispatch* the days in court were just beginning. The corporation that owns both papers, Richmond Newspapers, Inc., asked the Virginia appellate court to find that Judge Taylor was in error in closing the Stevenson trial. On July 9, 1979, the Virginia Supreme Court dismissed the appeal finding that no error had been made. In its opinion the Virginia court cited the United States Supreme Court decision in *Gannett v. DePasquale* that had been issued just the week before. The Virginia court apparently accepted one of the many plausible conclusions that could be drawn from the confusing opinions in that case—there is no public right to a public trial. Richmond Newspapers promptly appealed to the United States Supreme Court which agreed to hear the case. Because of the recent Gannett case whose confusing opinions were viewed as adding up to an anti-press decision, *Richmond Newspapers v. Virginia* attracted a lot of attention. Press organizations that presented arguments in support of the Richmond newspapers included the Reporters Committee for Freedom of the Press, the Associated Press Managing Editors, the National Association of Broadcasters, the National Newspaper Association, the National Press Club, the Radio-Television News Directors Association, the Society of Professional Journalists—Sigma Delta Chi, and the Virginia Press Association. Rather than suggest that there might be any conflict between the First and Sixth Amendments, these organizations and Richmond Newspapers argued that both amendments required that trials be public.

This case also gave the United States Supreme Court an opportunity to clear up the confusion that had been created by the majority opinions in the case of the Gannett Company's suit against Judge DePasquale decided the year before. In that decision the court majority appeared to agree that the Sixth Amendment right to a public trial was a right that belonged to the accused rather than to the public at large. However, the majority justices did not state clearly whether their support for secret judicial proceedings applied to all such proceedings or only pretrial hearings concerning the suppression of evidence. The Virginia courts read the *Gannett* opinions as a blanket permission to close all proceedings.

The Supreme Court heard oral arguments in the case on February 19, 1980, and issued its decision on July 2. By a vote of seven to one the Court ruled that Judge Richard H. C. Taylor had acted improperly in excluding the press and public from John Paul Stevenson's fourth trial for the murder of Lillian Keller. While they agreed about the conclusion, the majority justices did not agree about the reasons for this conclusion. The seven produced six separate opinions with no more than three justices supporting any one view.

The lead opinion for the majority was written by Chief Justice Warren Burger, whose view was supported by Justices Byron White and John Stevens. That opinion reviewed the lengthy history of the concept of public trial in Anglo-American jurisprudence, a review that echoed the detailed legal history written in his dissenting opinion in the *Gannett* case by Justice Harry Blackmun. However, unlike Justice Blackmun, the chief justice did not use this analysis to support the view that the public had a Sixth Amendment interest in a public trial. He had rejected that view in the *Gannett* case. Rather, the chief justice used the First Amendment guarantee of freedom of the press and the reserved rights clause of the Ninth Amendment as the constitutional basis for the traditional concept of a public trial. He found that the guarantees of these amendments "prohibit government from summarily closing courtroom doors which had long been open to the public at the time that amendment was adopted." The chief justice concluded his opinion by once again drawing the distinction

between a trial and a pretrial hearing—the distinction that was
the core of his concurring opinion in the *Gannett* case.

The five concurring opinions reflected the inability of the majority justices to agree on the reasons for their position. Justice
White, who had joined the lead opinion, observed that while he
agreed with the chief justice's First and Ninth Amendment anal-
sis, the whole "case would have been unnecessary" if the Court
had agreed with White's position in the *Gannett* case. Justice
Stevens' opinion called attention to the fact that the Court in this
case was recognizing for the first time that the press had a First
Amendment right to acquire newsworthy matter. Justice William
Brennan, writing for himself and Justice Thurgood Marshall,
stated that, without regard to the Sixth Amendment guarantee of
public trial, the First Amendment was more than sufficient to
prohibit closing a trial to the public. He supported his position
with an extensive historical analysis of the concept of public trial
and the First Amendment. Justice Potter Stewart supported the
outcome in this case because the trial judge had failed to conduct
a hearing to determine that a threat to fair trial existed prior to
ordering the closed trial. Finally, Justice Blackmun repeated his
view developed at length in the *Gannett* case to the effect that the
Sixth Amendment was both the sufficient and the best grounds
for upholding the public right to a public trial.

The single dissenting justice was William Rhenquist, who began his opinion by accusing Justices Burger and Brennan of cre-
ating new constitutional law in this case. He went on to restate
his position in the *Gannett* case that the Sixth Amendment right
to a public trial belonged to the accused and no one else. He
concluded this opinion as follows:

> The issue here is not whether the "right" to freedom of
> the press conferred by the First Amendment to the Consti-
> tution overrides the defendant's "right" to a fair trial con-

ferred by other amendments to the Constitution; it is instead whether any provision in the Constitution may fairl be read to prohibit what the trial judge in the Virginia state court system did in this case. Being unable to find any such prohibition in the First, Sixth, Ninth, or any other Amendments to the United States Constitution, or in the Constitution itself, I dissent.

The ninth justice, Lewis Powell, did not participate in th case. Justice Powell is from Virginia, had had a large private la practice, and had been active in the Virginia Bar Association pric to his appointment to the United States Supreme Court. As result, he was acquainted with several of those involved in th case. For this reason Justice Powell felt that it would be ethicall improper for him to take any part in the consideration or decisio in this case. This action was not unusual. United States Suprem Court justices normally are extremely sensitive to ethical que tions involved in their participation in any case and are quick t excuse themselves if there is even the slightest question abou their participation.

From the welter of opinions in the *Gannett* and *Richmon Newspapers* cases, it is possible to draw some general conclusion First, for whatever reason the public as well as the defendant ha a constitutional right to a public trial. Second, the pretrial phase of the judicial process, particularly pretrial hearings on the ac missibility of evidence, may be treated differently than the tri itself if circumstances demand such treatment. Specifically, may be possible to protect a defendant's Sixth Amendment rigl to a fair trial by limiting the flow of information to the publ through the devise of a closed pretrial evidentiary hearing.

CHAPTER 7

Cameras in the Courtroom
Is Someone Trying to Kill Sunny?

Perhaps more than any other place in America Newport, Rhode Island, with its row of multimillion-
dollar summer cottages is the home of the very rich
and often famous. Few were more well known than
heiress Martha ("Sunny") Crawford (von Auersperg) von Bülow,
who lived at Clarendon Court, one of those places (like the White
House) where the mail gets delivered even though there is no
street address.

On December 27, 1979, an ambulance was called to Clarendon
Court by Claus von Bülow, Sunny's current husband. The medical technicians found Sunny lying unconscious on her bed. She
was having apparent difficulty breathing. Dr. Janis Gailitas
administered cardiopulmonary resuscitation at the scene, and
Sunny was rushed to Newport Hospital where the doctors worked
successfully to regularize her breathing and restore her to consciousness.

A year later, on December 21, 1980, the ambulance made a
return trip to Clarendon Court. This time Sunny was found
unconscious on the marble floor of her bathroom, and, in spite of
all the efforts by the Newport Hospital staff, she has never
regained consciousness.

These events with their serious consequences required an
explanation. Claus von Bülow's account of the events was that in
1979, following an argument concerning his desire for a divorce
to marry another woman, Sunny had consumed several eggnogs

and taken barbiturates. Her unconscious state was the result of this combination. The second event was the result of an advers reaction to a combination of pills that Sunny had taken.

Sunny von Bülow's two children from a prior marriage foun these explanations less than satisfactory. The children hired former New York City prosecutor, Richard Kuh, to investigat the circumstances surrounding their mother's two Christmas time comas. Their suspicions had been fed by their mother maid, Maria Schrallhammer, who had reported finding a blac bag in their stepfather's closet that contained drugs and a vial c insulin. Investigator Kuh found the bag and a needle that, whe tested, showed traces of insulin. The children's explanation wa that their mother's comas were the result of unnecessary insuli injections given by their stepfather, Claus, in attempts to kill hi wife.

As might be expected with the rich and famous, money was central matter of controversy. Who would have inherited th multimillion-dollar estate as the result of Sunny von Bülow death? Claus would receive $14 million besides the $2 millio trust fund that Sunny had already given him. In addition t money there was sex. It was widely known that Bülow was not faithful husband and was carrying on an affair with at least or other woman.

In this situation it is not surprising that the children went to th police with their suspicions and evidence with the result that th state of Rhode Island indicted Claus von Bülow on two counts c attempted murder. The six-week trial in Newport in 1982 re ceived, as would be expected, extensive media coverage. Sunny maid, Maria, testified that she asked, "Insulin. What for insu lin?" when she found the black bag, and these words were sprea across the nation. Alexandra Isles, Bülow's mistress and by th point a well-known character in the drama, testified that short before the first coma she had threatened to leave him if he did n divorce Sunny. Medical evidence was presented that insulin ha been found in blood samples taken when Sunny was admitted to the hospital in 1980. Given this case, the public that had eagerly followed the details of the trial was not surprised when the jury found Bülow guilty, and he was sentenced to thirty years in prison.

One major legal advantage of the rich is their financial capacity to appeal adverse court decisions, and Claus von Bülow appealed. To assist in this effort he secured the services of a well-known Harvard law professor, Alan Dershowitz. The argument Dershowitz presented to the Rhode Island Supreme Court was that the prosecution had improperly withheld evidence from the defense and that the trial judge had allowed inadmissible evidence to be presented to the jury. For example, a copy of the notes on the case made by private investigator Kuh had never been provided to Bülow's defense attorneys. The court responded favorably to these arguments, reversed Bülow's conviction, and ordered a new trial.

As was seen in the several trials of John Paul Stevenson, retrial after a reversal of conviction compounds the problems of pretrial publicity, a situation especially true in the case of a celebrity defendant such as Claus von Bülow. The first step taken to provide Bülow with an impartial jury was change of venue, to move the trial from Newport to Providence, Rhode Island. While the distance is only thirty-five miles, Providence offered better courtroom facilities and the jury pool of the largest city in the state. Loud objections were heard from the business community of Newport, which was looking forward to the off-season bonanza of tourists that the new trial would attract.

At the outset of the new trial which began in April 1985, Corrine P. Grande, the trial court judge assigned to the case, made clear her concern about providing Bülow a fair trial. The magnitude of the problem was shown when Judge Grande asked the first panel of about seventy prospective jurors how many had heard about the case. Hands were raised by almost everyone. She rephrased the question to ask how many had not heard, and only five hands were raised. When asked, several indicated that they had formed an opinion about the case. Thus began a two-week process of extensive voir dire examination that led to the selection of eleven women and five men who were the twelve jurors and four alternates that would decide the facts of the case.

While the jury selection process was going on, Judge Grande, the prosecutors, and Bülow's trial attorney, well-known former federal prosecutor Thomas Puccio, debated whether to sequester the jury. In a seeming reversal of usual positions the prosecutor argued for sequestering, while Puccio argued against it even to the point of promising never to raise the issue of prejudicial publicity on appeal if his client were once again convicted. In the end Judge Grande decided that the jury would be sequestered because, as she observed, "The amount and kind of potentially inadmissible and prejudicial evidence in this case is very much like a time bomb ticking away. If it goes off, it will destroy the right of both parties to a fair trial."

One last issue remained to be resolved before the trial could begin: What to do with all the reporters seeking to cover the trial for an eager public. Judge Grande assigned 33 of the 135 seats in the courtroom to specific news organizations that requested space. Additional seats were taken on a daily basis by other reporters and photographers. Some two hundred news media people were present in Providence for the trial. Friends and family of Claus von Bülow and Sunny's two children also claimed space, so that sometimes as few as 30 seats were left for the general public that lined up to claim them as much as ninety minutes before the courtroom doors opened.

And then there was television. In *Estes v. Texas* in 1965 the United States Supreme Court had considered the broadcasting of pretrial activity in a notorious case and had concluded in an opinion written by Justice Tom Clark that these broadcasts had fatal impact on Estes' right to a fair trial. Although the Court eemed to have decided the issue against broadcasting, many tates continued to experiment with the use of television cameras n the courtroom. Over the years broadcasting technology improved enough that the sideshow of lights, cables, generators, nd huge cameras that Clark described in the *Estes* case opinion vas no longer a factor.

In 1981 a case coming out of Florida, *Chandler v. Florida*, ave the Court an opportunity to reconsider its position on elevision broadcasting of legal proceedings. In this case a ormer police officer convicted of burglary asked that his conviction be reversed because portions of his trial seen by an inconpicuous courtroom television camera had appeared on news roadcasts about the trial. In refusing to reverse, the Court drew distinction between modern broadcast technology and the ituation in the *Estes* case. The conclusion was that television roadcasting does not automatically undermine fair trial rights f a defendant.

Following the Chandler decision new laws were passed in a najority of states lifting the bar on cameras in the courtroom. elevision coverage of at least portions of trials on regular news rograms became common. Full coverage of the often-tedious roceedings of a complete trial was rare. One notable exception o this rule was the coverage by the Cable News Network (CNN) f a rape trial in New Bedford, Massachusetts. The case had ained national prominence because of the nature of the attack nd became known as the Big Dan rape case from the name of the ar in which the attack took place.

Because of the intense national interest in the case, the Claus on Bülow retrial was a natural for CNN, and Rhode Island was ne of the states that permitted the broadcasting of trials. Thus te network requested, and Judge Grande granted to it, the right o broadcast nationally live coverage of the trial with the possibility of rebroadcasting whatever portions they might wish. ince the cameras and microphones would be unobtrusive and the jury was sequestered, Judge Grande apparently concluded that this coverage would not interfere with Bülow's right to a fair trial but would help satisfy the clear, strong public interest in the event.

For CNN the decision to broadcast was a good business decision. Audience size as determined by the rating services was good. "The Claus von Bülow Retrial" logo used for each broadcast segment was effective, and ad sales were brisk (although CNN was deluged with complaint calls from viewers when they interrupted trial testimony for commercials). Many television viewers turned from the soap operas to watch this real life soap complete with testimony by Bülow's former mistress, Alexandra Isles, whose prior television exposure had been as an actress on one of the fictional afternoon soaps, *Dark Shadows.*

In addition the CNN viewers were able to watch much to which the actual trial jurors were never exposed. They saw the comings and goings of Bülow, his new mistress, and Sunny's children — only one of whom ever appeared on the witness stand. They saw many of the courtroom debates when the jury was not present about admissibility of evidence. They heard commentators discuss the significance of the outcomes of these debates as well as differences, consistencies, and inconsistencies in the evidence presented in Bülow's first trial and the second one. They saw the crowds around the courthouse wearing "Free Claus" tee shirts.

One print media acknowledgment of the extent to which the CNN coverage penetrated public consciousness can be seen in the trial trivia quiz run by *The Eagle,* a Providence free-distribution alternative weekly. Only a diligent watcher of the trial on CNN could answer the questions such as the color of Judge Grande's eyeglasses frames (the answer: red on a color set and gray on a black-and-white set).

Beyond the reach of all the media hoopla the jury received the case after a seven-week trial on which the defendant was estimated to have spent as much as a million dollars. The jury found

Claus von Bülow not guilty of attempting to murder his wife. The nationwide television audience/jury may or may not have reached a different conclusion. But whatever the viewers' opinions might be, they had experienced a massive media event in which the actual trial had only been a part, and that event continued. On the evening the verdict was announced, Ted Koppel, on his show *Nightline,* hosted a lively debate about the trial and its outcome, and three days later Bülow appeared for a live interview with Barbara Walters on *20/20* (both American Broadcasting Company network programs).

While the CNN coverage of the trial was the most extensive, television was not the only medium through which trial events were communicated to the public. All those reporters with their assigned courtroom seats filed stories that appeared regularly in the world's newspapers and news magazines. For example, *The New York Times* carried almost daily stories that typically were some twenty column inches long. Of course on the morning following Bülow's acquittal the recap story was almost a full page in length. The Providence papers carried full-page stories with large pictures daily.

In addition there were books. Following the first trial *The von Bülow Affair,* by William Wright, had been a best-selling paperback for Dell Publishing. It supported the jury verdict in that trial. After the second trial Alan Dershowitz wrote *Reversal of Fortune,* published by Random House, that went on to become a popular 1990 film of the same name in which the star, Jeremy Irons, won the Academy Award for best actor for his portrayal of Claus von Bülow.

The 1932 kidnap and murder of the infant son of world hero Charles Lindbergh was a major public tragedy referred to at the time as the crime of the century. The trial three years later of Bruno Richard Hauptmann for this crime was the news media circus of the century. Reaction within the legal community to the abuses and excesses of this event led directly to the development of rules designed to prevent such spectacles in the future by prohibiting the use of cameras in the courtroom. For some forty years the only pictures of trials seen in print media or on television were the sketches of artists used to compensate for the absent camera.

Rapid and extensive improvements in the 1970s in the technology of image capture and transmission led to reconsideration in some jurisdictions of the absolute ban on cameras. A variety of experiments seemed to demonstrate that cameras do not necessarily produce the excesses of the Hauptmann trial. Finally, as noted earlier, the Supreme Court of the United States in 1981 concluded that the presence of cameras and broadcast of trials does not automatically mean that the trial is unfair.

The second attempted-murder trial of Claus von Bülow provides a good test of the impact of cameras and broadcasting on the fair trial rights of a defendant. Regardless of whether one agrees or disagrees with the second trial outcome, there is no evidence that the extensive trial coverage, particularly the live CNN broadcasting of the proceedings, affected that outcome. A number of factors contributed to this result.

First, there were the traditional remedies of continuance and change of venue. The second trial came three years after the first trial and over four years after the alleged crime. The location of the trial was moved from the community in which the alleged crime took place to the largest city in the state.

The second group of factors involved the jury. A large panel of prospective jurors was subjected to careful voir dire examination that led to the selection of sixteen apparently impartial jurors. Once selected, this group was sequestered and thus shielded from the extensive news media coverage of the trial. The unobtrusive cameras and microphones in the courtroom do not seem to have been a distraction.

In some jurisdictions, particularly the federal courts, cameras of all kinds are still banned. Some lawyers, judges, and legisla ors continue to believe that the presence of cameras would have undesirable effects on courtroom practices. The second trial of Claus von Bülow seems to demonstrate that these fears are unfounded. A careful and thoughtful judge using traditional methods can assure a fair trial for a defendant no matter how extensive public curiosity and news reporting may be.

CHAPTER 8

Ethical Guidelines
for Crime Reporting
The Saga of a Serial Killer

O ne of the principal activities of news organizations is the reporting of crimes. Crime stories make up a substantial portion of both print and broadcast news, and in any larger metropolitan area there is consistently much to report. The Rochester, New York, metropolitan area is a representative example with its daily quota of robbery, assault, shooting, rape, and/or violent death. Killings, for instance, occur in the area a little more often than twice a month.

Among the deaths reported during the years 1986 to 1989 approximately eighteen were deaths in which the victims were young women whose often partially clad bodies had been found along a riverbank, in woods or a weed lot, or behind a deserted building. In many of these cases there appeared to be a connection with prostitution and/or drug use. Coming as they did over time and interspersed among all the other killings reported, these cases did not attract any special notice until fall 1989 when several bodies were discovered within a short period of time. Police began to tie the women's deaths together, and the local morning newspaper, the Gannett *Democrat and Chronicle*, began to report on the apparent connection of the deaths in stories that appeared under a repeated headline often in red, "The Serial Slayings Victims of the Street." Both this paper and Gannett's evening *Times-Union* published lengthy articles beginning on page one and carrying over to two full inside pages describing, complete with pictures, the lives and deaths of each of the seemingly connected murder victims. (It should be noted that Rochester is not a competitive newspaper market. Both papers are owned by the Gannett chain and share offices, facilities, and even complete editorial sections.)

Once the idea of a connection among the deaths led to the supposition that a serial killer was at work in the area, hardly a day went by without some news story related to the subject. For example, under the large headline "Outraged About the Violence" a B-section first-page story that ran in the December 19, 1989, *Democrat and Chronicle* reported on a gathering of seventy people at the Rochester Institute of Technology to protest violence against women. Another story about a group that was proposing the opening of a safe house for prostitutes also received the same B-section treatment complete with the added "Serial Slayings" caption.

On December 31, 1989, clothing found in a Monroe County park on the west side of Rochester was identified as belonging to a woman who had been reported missing. The police search for the woman was fully reported by all local news organizations. By this time the multiple killings had received so much notice that a story on this possible new victim even appeared in *The New York Times*. When the snow that had covered the ground melted, the police found the woman's body, and the headline on the front page of the *Democrat and Chronicle* proclaimed "Another Corpse Is Found." Not to be outdone the *Times-Union* ran an extra B-section article of fifty-six column inches, including pictures, under the head "Dogs with the Scents to Track Bodies." In sum, by the first week in January 1990, it would have been hard to find anyone in the Rochester metropolitan area who had not been exposed to at least some reporting about these multiple killings.

On January 4, 1990, a series of chance events led to the arrest of Arthur Shawcross, who was charged with several of the unsolved killings. The next day the *Times-Union* filled almost the entire front page and two full inside pages with stories complete with pictures of the accused and several of his alleged victims. The main headline proclaimed, "Parolee Charged as Serial Killer of 8."

The news reports on January 5 set the tone for what was to follow on almost a daily basis. The fourth paragraph of the *Times-Union*'s lead article said,

> Shawcross, 241 Alexander Street, who was on parole for killing an 8-year-old Rochester girl and a 10-year-old Watertown boy in 1972, was being questioned about the deaths of at least 14 women and the disappearance of two others over the last two years.

The story went on to say that Shawcross had admitted involvement in the eight deaths noted in the story's headline. A second front-page article under the headline "Family, Friends Report a Stormy Past" included the following:

> Seventeen years ago, Arthur John Shawcross, then a Watertown Public Works Department laborer, pleaded guilty to a first-degree manslaughter charge for the sexual assault and strangulation of 8-year-old Karen Ann Hill and the death of 10-year-old Jack O. Blake of Watertown.
>
> The deaths of the two children followed a number of arrests for snowball fights with children, the arson fire at a milk plant where he worked, a tour of duty in Vietnam and a two-year stint in Attica [a New York State maximum security prison] on a burglary charge.
>
> . . . .
>
> In Sept., 1972, young Karen Ann Hill, a Rochester girl who had been visiting Watertown with her mother, Helene

Hill, was raped and strangled a block from the Jefferson County home where they were staying.

···

During police questioning about the killing, Shawcross also confessed to another murder, that of Blake.

···

Shawcross confessed to Blake's murder in court for a reduced manslaughter conviction on Oct. 17, 1972 on the theory he was suffering from "extreme emotional disturbance," according to newspaper accounts. Shawcross was sentenced to and [*sic*] indeterminate amount of time of not more than 25 years.

Shawcross was released on parole in April 1987, but not without problems.

Shawcross was to relocate in Binghamton where he would serve his parole, but Binghamton residents vociferously protested the move. He settled with a girlfriend in an apartment in the Jefferson County village of Delhi. The girlfriend was evicted in June of 1987. Shawcross left town that month ans [*sic*] moved to Rochester.

These initial reports about Arthur Shawcross' prior criminal record were followed with much more detailed stories about his psychological state. On January 8, under the three-color caption "The Serial Slayings Victims of the Street" on the front page of the *Democrat and Chronicle,* the lead sentence of the story said, "As details of the crimes attributed to accused serial killer Arthur J. Shawcross come to light, psychologists and psychiatrists are able to paint a portrait of a highly troubled man for whom the chilling label of 'psychopath' fits well." The story related interviews with three mental health professionals from around the country—none of whom had examined Shawcross— in which Shawcross was described as a "psychopath," "not a true pedophile," an "organized killer" like other serial killers such as John Wayne Gacy and Ted Bundy, and a person whose basic motive was murder rather than sex. The next day the front-page story, again using the three-color "Serial Slayings" caption, provided a detailed description of Shawcross' rape and murder of Karen Ann Hill in 1972. This story, with a supporting article, pictures, and reproductions of old newspaper stories, ran more than a hundred column inches.

On January 12, the *Democrat and Chronicle* reported on page 1 Shawcross' first court appearance and indictment using the three-color "Serial Slayings" caption and two large pictures of Shawcross, whose face was by now a familiar feature on television and in the newspapers. The day's second story dealt with speculation about Shawcross' possible connection with killings in Pennsylvania and Ohio. Also on this day the degree to which the details of the story had penetrated public consciousness was illustrated by letters to the editor filling two-thirds of a page in both papers—including two pictures of Shawcross. The letters questioned why Shawcross was paroled, and several demanded restoration of the death penalty.

Throughout the month of January 1990, stories appeared on almost a daily basis in both newspapers, usually on the front page of either the A or B section and often with a picture of Shawcross. The *Democrat and Chronicle* consistently used its "Serial Slayings" caption in three colors. Almost any detail, including a change in assigned defense lawyers and the clearing of Shawcross as a suspect in the killings in other states, justified a story. Most of these stories reviewed Shawcross' status as a convicted and paroled killer. On January 13, *The New York Times* joined in with a story at the top of the second section that reviewed Shawcross' prior criminal record and discussed his psychological state. A second story dealt with criticism of the parole system by Monroe County District Attorney Howard Relin.

Given the extent and nature of the publicity surrounding the case, it is not surprising that on January 17 assigned defense lawyer David Murante asked the Monroe County court judge overseeing the case to issue an order that would forbid prosecutors, law enforcement officials, and defense lawyers from talking to reporters. Murante observed that "I don't know how my client can expect at this time to receive a fair trial" given the pervasive national and local media attention the case had received. This request, the objection by the district attorney's office, and the judge's denial of the request were all duly reported in the *Times-Union* the next day. The *Times-Union* also ran a twenty-two column-inch article based on an examination of public documents that recounted Shawcross' life as a model prisoner during his sixteen years in the Green Haven Correctional Facility. This story detailed Shawcross' prison life, his several appearances before the parole board, and his psychiatric treatment and adjustment.

On January 26, the *Times-Union* reported that all four of the local network affiliate television stations as well as the local cable company's public access channel had requested permission to broadcast Shawcross' eventual trial. Both the *Democrat and Chronicle* and the *Times-Union* had asked for permission to take still photographs. Such coverage was then allowed in New York State with the permission of the trial judge. In response to these requests the trial judge, Donald Wisner, allowed the trial to be covered with two television cameras and two still cameras. The commercial broadcasters presented excerpts on their news shows, and the local public access cable channel broadcast the entire trial live. The newspapers that had regularly published photographs of virtually every court appearance by Shawcross ran photos of the trial on almost a daily basis.

After a couple of months of relative quiet, the start of the Shawcross trial in mid-September produced a new frenzy of publicity. Front-page stories with jumps to full-page coverage inside appeared in both Gannett papers. The process of jury selection was covered extensively. An initial panel of three thousand was reduced through a questionnaire examination process to a thousand, and these thousand were subjected to extensive questioning in groups of twenty-one by the judge and prosecution and defense attorneys. There appeared to be good cooperation among the three in excusing anyone who any of the three found worrisome. On September 27, the *Democrat and Chronicle* reported the results of the process with profiles of the twelve jurors and four alternates. In a self-proclaimed demonstration of responsible journalism the names of the sixteen were not included, although the profile details would seem to make them readily identifiable by friends and associates. The jury was not sequestered.

A central topic in the September Shawcross publicity was the intention of the defense to mount an insanity defense. This development led to still another review of Shawcross' life, this time with special attention to his experience as a veteran of the Vietnam War. It was also reported for the first time on September 17, in the *Times-Union,* that Shawcross had been sexually abused as a child. At the end of the month the district attorney, Howard Relin, gave an interview in which he discredited the idea of an insanity defense that resulted in a front-page story in the September 30 *Times-Union* headlined "Insanity Case a Tough Sell for Defense." This interview and resulting newspaper story just after the jury had been sworn was finally enough for Judge Wisner, who at long last granted the defense motion for a gag order to be applied to all the officers of the court.

A second major pretrial issue was that of the alleged confessions that Shawcross had made. The defense sought to establish that Shawcross had been tricked and not informed of his rights. Thus, the written and videotaped confessions should not be admitted as evidence. Judge Wisner ruled against these defense motions, but the issue appeared to be almost irrelevant, since the content of these confessions had already been reported in full. In fact, the local public broadcasting station reported on the day that the jury was sworn that it had been contacted by "documentary producers" offering to sell copies of the videotaped confessions for $10,000. Similar offers had apparently been made to the commercial stations, but there were no buyers. The tapes would, of course, be broadcast when introduced in the trial.

From all this almost daily extensive and intensive reporting about Arthur Shawcross few in the Rochester media market, apparently including the trial jurors and alternates, could have avoided knowing about this case. Certainly the case had become the crime story of at least the decade. The information provided by the news stories included the following:

1. The names, pictures, and biographies of many killing victims including several for which Shawcross was not charged

2. The identification, complete with multiple pictures, of Shawcross as the accused

3. Reports that Shawcross had confessed to several of the killings, with complete details of those confessions

4. Extensive and repeated discussion of Shawcross' past criminal record

5. Extended discussion of, and speculation about, Shawcross' psychological make-up including speculation about the possible use of an insanity defense

Cases such as the *Shawcross* present the fundamental problem of the apparent conflict between the constitutional right of news agencies to report freely whatever they wish and the constitutional right of a defendant to receive a fair trial. The basic idea of a fair trial is that the case should be decided by an impartial jury exclusively on the evidence presented during the trial free of any prior or external influences.

One approach to resolving the seeming conflict between freedom of the press and the right to a fair trial has been the development of ethical rules of conduct often referred to as press-bar guidelines because of their origin in conferences between lawyers and journalists. The real horror story of press coverage of the *Sheppard* case led to a number of considerations by both bar and press associations of ways to deal with the free press–fair trial conflict. Beginning with the recommendations of the American Bar Association's Advisory Committee on Free Press/Fair Trial in 1966 and amplified by numerous joint press-bar association guidelines, agreements have been developed regarding materials that as an ethical principle should be left out of crime reports. These included the following:

1. An accused's prior criminal record
2. Reporting any purported confessions
3. Results of any tests, physical or psychological, that might have been conducted
4. Review of or speculation about the mental state of the accused

There appears to be general agreement that reporting these matters would be inherently prejudicial to the fair trial rights of the accused.

While the specifics of press-bar guidelines vary from place to place, the four items listed above are common features. These were the elements in the Nebraska press-bar guidelines that Judges Ruff and Stuart sought to impose by court order in the Kellie murder case discussed in chapter 4. In New York State a group called the New York Fair Trial Free Press Conference, chaired by Sol Wachtler, chief judge of the Court of Appeals (the name given to New York's highest court), has produced and published a set of principles and guidelines outlined below.

All should be aware of the dangers of prejudice in making pretrial disclosure of the following:

(a) Statements as to the character or reputation of an accused person or a prospective witness.

(b) Admissions, confessions or the contents of a statement or alibi attributable to an accused person.

(c) The performance or results of tests or the refusal of the accused to take a test.

. . . .

(e) The possibility of a plea of guilty to the offense charged or to a lesser offense, or other disposition.

(f) Opinions concerning evidence or argument in the case, whether or not it is anticipated that such evidence or argument will be used at trial.

Prior criminal charges and convictions are matters of public record. . . . The public disclosure of this information by news media may be highly prejudicial without any significant addition to the public's need to be informed. The publication of such information should be carefully considered by the news media.

When the handling of the *Shawcross* case by the Rochester market news media, and even *The New York Times*, is measured against these New York State crime-reporting recommendations, major indiscretions abound. In this noncompetitive newspaper market both Gannett papers decided to report extensively on Shawcross' purported confessions. His prior criminal record became the focus of a number of longer stories. Reporters sought out public records and experts around the nation to report on and speculate about Shawcross' mental state. There was much speculation about a not-guilty-by-reason-of-insanity plea and the possibilities of the success of such a plea. In sum, the news reporting in no way matched the voluntary press-bar guidelines for appropriate crime reporting.

The lesson of the *Shawcross* case is that while recommended ethical principles for crime reporting might go a long way toward protecting an accused's right to a fair trial, they will be ignored by news organizations pursuing a story in which there is real or media-manufactured public interest. As Shawcross defense attorney David Morante observed, "I don't know how my client can expect at this time to receive a fair trial" given the way the case had been reported by the news media.

If we accept the premise that real freedom of the press is the freedom to be as irresponsible as the press chooses, it is obvious that responsible conduct—even if we could agree on the meaning of the term—cannot be compelled. The performance of agencies reporting the news in the *Shawcross* and other major crime cases demonstrate that in the real world unenforceable voluntary guidelines for ethical crime reporting will be ignored. If Arthur Shawcross or other criminal defendants are to receive a fair trial, they must look to something other than the voluntary ethical standards of press-bar guidelines to protect that right. The mechanisms for resolving conflicts between a free press and a fair trial must be found elsewhere.

CHAPTER 9

The First and the Sixth

In the preceding pages the stories of seven different murder cases have been presented. Unlike most criminal prosecutions, each of these cases generated some public attention. The trial of Sam Sheppard would, in the normal course of events, attract public attention because of Sheppard's professional and social prominence. The natural interest was exploited both by politicians seeking votes and by newspapers seeking increased circulation. The trial of Charles Manson and his followers was guaranteed to attract public attention because of the bizarre nature of the crimes and the fact that one victim was a famous Hollywood movie star. Even in a large city a multiple murder such as that committed by Erwin Simants, particularly one that also involved sexual assault, would attract some public attention even though both the murderer and his victims were unknown. However, in a thinly populated rural area such a crime would be a major event of direct interest and concern for almost everyone. Although Wayne Clapp had some public status as a former police officer and had disappeared in a rural area, general public interest in his case was not as widespread. For John Paul Stevenson the repeated murder trials were one of those unusual events that attracts the attention of a curious public. The retrial of Claus von Bülow for the attempted murder of his wife was a major television event—a real-life soap opera. The crimes of Arthur Shawcross, like those of other serial killers, received extensive news coverage.

In each of these seven cases the trial court judge had the obligation to assure that the defendants received a fair trial in which an impartial jury could reach a decision based on the trial evidence uninfluenced by other information. In the case of Sam Sheppard, Judge Blythin, except for occasional and minimal admonishments to the jury, ignored his responsibilities in this area. In contrast the trial of the Manson group was marked by the use by the trail judge of just about every means at his disposal to secure and maintain an impartial jury. Within four days of the Kellie murders Judge Ruff recognized that there might be a problem securing an impartial jury and took steps to control the flow of information that could be prejudicial to the defendant. On the grounds that a defendant gains little or nothing by being able to suppress evidence that is then reported by the news media, Judge DePasquale excluded the press and public from a pretrial hearing on the suppression of evidence. In response to a defense request at the beginning of John Paul Stevenson's fourth trial on the charge that he murdered Lillian Keller, Judge Taylor excluded the press and public from the trial itself as a necessary step to assure Stevenson a fair trial. While allowing almost unprecedented television coverage, Judge Grande took care to shield the jurors in the Bülow retrial from this broadcasting and all the other extensive news reporting. In the *Shawcross* case the influence on the trial outcome of the massive pretrial publicity is not known, nor is it known how carefully the jury obeyed Judge Wisner's instructions to avoid the television broadcasting and all other reporting during the trial.

Higher courts have reacted in a variety of ways to these efforts, or lack thereof, by trial court judges. In the *Sheppard* case the United States Supreme Court eventually ruled that he had been deprived of even the minimal requirements of a fair trial by the repeated acts and omissions of Judge Blythin. The opinion written by Justice Tom Clark contains a catalog of the techniques that can be used by a trial judge to obtain an impartial jury and guarantee a fair trial.

1. Because all law enforcement officers and lawyers are officers of the court, a judge can issue orders controlling their

conduct. Specifically they can be ordered not to divulge any information concerning the case to the news media. Anyone failing to obey such an order would be guilty of contempt of court and could be fined or sent to prison.

2. If there has been extensive publicity and the defense requests it, a trial judge can grant a continuance which will postpone the trial to a later date (but in the near future) during which time the publicity may decline.

3. The defense can also request a change of venue to move the trial to some other location where jurors could be found that had not been influenced by the pretrial publicity.

4. Regardless of the time and location of the trial, extensive voir dire examination of jurors can be conducted. Such examinations designed to determine the extent of jurors' knowledge and prejudices about the case can make a major contribution toward securing an impartial jury for the defendant. As an additional precaution, the judge can clearly and forcefully instruct the jury that they are to decide the case on the basis of the evidence introduced in the trial and nothing else.

5. Once a jury has been selected, the trial judge can order them sequestered for the duration of the trial to assure that they are not subject to any outside influence. One problem with this technique is that it is a major inconvenience for the jurors who may then prejudice the outcome of the trial by blaming the defendant for this disruption of their lives.

In the *Sheppard* case the United States Supreme Court found that the trial court had failed to use the available techniques with the result that Sam Sheppard was denied his Sixth Amendment right to a fair trial. None of the techniques which should have been used would interfere with the First Amendment rights of the general public and news media. Justice Clark also recognized that the Supreme Court's review and reversal was not a satisfactory solution to the problem. That decision came twelve years after Sheppard's trial and conviction.

In the Tate-LaBianca murders case, trial Judge Charles Older made use of most of the techniques recommended in Justice Clark's opinion in the *Sheppard* case. All witnesses and court officers were ordered not to speak to reporters about the case. However, this order was less than totally successful because of repeated and anonymous violations by those with a variety of motives for the violations. Continuance and a change of venue were not used because Judge Older concluded that they would be of little value. An extensive voir dire examination of potential jurors was conducted, and the jury was sequestered for the duration of the lengthy trial. Meanwhile the news media were free to report whatever they wished, and they did. There were no successful First or Sixth Amendment appeals arising from this case.

The trial of Erwin Simants for the Kellie family murders presented a different problem. Much of the information that could jeopardize Simants' right to a fair trial was part of the public record in the case. In this situation Judges Ruff and Stuart concluded that the only way to protect Simants' rights was to prohibit the news media from publishing this public record. While they were sympathetic to the concerns of the Nebraska court, the United States Supreme Court found that the means used by that court violated the free press guarantee of the First Amendment. The order prohibiting publication was an unconstitutional prior restraint on freedom of the press. All the Supreme Court justices seem to agree that the traditional techniques outlined in the *Sheppard* case opinion, particularly a careful voir dire examination, would have been sufficient in this case.

One of the most difficult issues facing a judge in any criminal trial is that of deciding on the admissibility of evidence. The Bill of Rights contains a number of specific guarantees for those accused of criminal offenses. However, in an effort to secure the evidence needed to convict an accused, law enforcement officials and prosecutors sometimes violate these constitutional guaran tees. Such evidence cannot be admitted in a criminal trial. If the substance of nonadmissible evidence is reported to prospective jurors through the news media, has the purpose of the suppression of that evidence been defeated? That is the question that Judge DePasquale faced in a suppression hearing arising out of the disappearance of Wayne Clapp. Judge DePasquale held that to prevent possible prejudicial publication of the evidence the public and press could be excluded from the hearing, and the United States Supreme Court agreed. The majority of the Supreme Court found that the closure of such a hearing did not violate the First Amendment guarantee of freedom of the press.

It was precisely this problem of admissibility of evidence that led to the several trials of John Paul Stevenson. His conviction at his original murder trial was based in part on the evidence of his knit shirt with a blood stain. An appeals court found that this evidence should have been suppressed. After two mistrials because of problems within the jury, the defense asked at the outset of the fourth trial that the public and press be excluded because their presence was prejudicial to Stevenson's right to a fair trial. While the trial judge agreed to a hearing on the issue, he granted the defense request and continued that order after the hearing on the issue. After the prosecution presented its case at the closed trial, Judge Taylor ruled that the case against Stevenson was insufficient and that he should be found not guilty. The action of Judge Taylor in closing the trial as a means to assure a fair trial was considered by the United States Supreme Court, which decided with only one dissent that the press and public have a constitutional right based on the First and Ninth Amendments to be present at a trial. If the trial court would use the remedies outlined in the *Sheppard* case, there would be no need to exclude the press and public in order to assure a fair trial. No conflict between freedom of the press guaranteed by the First Amendment and the right to a fair trial guaranteed by the Sixth Amendment would then exist.

The public at large has always had a fascination for the lives of the rich and famous. Thus it was natural that the intrigues involving both money and sex in the trials of Claus von Bülow for the attempted murder of his wife received extensive media attention. With the reversal of the original conviction, the retrial received even greater attention. The task for Judge Grande was to find a way to satisfy the demands of the news media while at the same time assuring that the case would be heard by an impartial jury. To satisfy the first demand, cameras in the courtroom and live television broadcasting of the trial were permitted. Reporters were provided with the greatest possible access. The second demand was met by a change of venue for the trial and a very careful jury selection followed by sequestering so that the jury had only the evidence submitted to them in the courtroom to consider in reaching its verdict.

The trial of serial killer Arthur Shawcross presented a problematic situation. Extensive investigative reporting provided the public with detailed information about the accused. Few details of his life from early childhood to the time the trial began were not extensively reported. While the judge, prosecution, and defense sought through voir dire examination to select an impartial jury, the jurors who decided the case had all been exposed to at least some of the highly prejudicial information that appeared in the community's newspapers on an almost daily basis. In addition the jury was not sequestered and thus was very possibly exposed to the continued extensive newspaper and broadcast coverage of the trial, which included a local cable channel's live broadcast of the trial. The observer is left to wonder what part all this exposure might have played in the jury's decision to reject the insanity defense and find Shawcross guilty of murder.

These seven cases have illustrated the range of problems that exemplify the free press/fair trial issue. They can be read to suggest that there is a fundamental conflict between the rights guaranteed by the First Amendment and those guaranteed by the

Sixth Amendment. The role of the United States Supreme Court is to balance these conflicting claims in the cases that come before it. However, a more careful analysis reveals that this conflict is more an illusion than real. Justice Clark's opinion in the *Sheppard* case explained the tools that could be used to protect Sixth Amendment rights without interfering with First Amendment rights, and the Tate-LaBianca murders case illustrated the effective use of those tools. In the Wayne Clapp case Judge DePasquale developed an additional Sixth Amendment tool, which the United States Supreme Court decided did not interfere with First Amendment rights. Other judges responding to particular problems have used other techniques, but the United States Supreme Court has found them improper both because they were not needed to guarantee a defendant's Sixth Amendment right to a fair trial and because they were a violation of the First Amendment right of freedom of speech and press.

The recent history of criminal trials in the United States suggests that judges are more aware of their First and Sixth Amendment responsibilities and, particularly in cases attracting great public attention, do a good job of protecting constitutional rights under both these amendments. For example, the available evidence indicates that James Earl Ray who killed Martin Luther King, Jr., Sirhan Sirhan who murdered Senator Robert F. Kennedy, and John Hinckley, Jr., who shot President Ronald Reagan all received fair trials and were judged by impartial juries. Their Sixth Amendment rights were not jeopardized by the news media's exercise of First Amendment rights.

The preceding observations should not, however, lead the reader to the conclusion that all conflicts have been resolved. Very real problems remain. The guarantees of the First Amendment are rights rather than privileges—rights that remain intact (with few exceptions) regardless of how they are used. The news media are not required to act responsibly, and occasionally they do not. As we saw in the Tate-LaBianca murders, and in the

Claus von Bülow and *Shawcross* cases, competition and profit motives can lead to media behavior that increases the difficulty of securing a fair trial for those accused of crimes. Members of the bar can also engage in behavior that impairs a defendant's chance for a fair trial.

On the media side a recent example of this behavior can be seen in the trial of John Z. Delorean, an auto executive accused of conspiring to possess and distribute fifty-five pounds of cocaine. The major evidence for the prosecution in this case was videotapes made secretly of what were said to be drug meetings. Prior to the trial a law clerk made a copy of the tapes and sold them to Larry Flynt, the publisher of *Hustler* magazine, who in turn sold the material to the Columbia Broadcasting System for use on their popular news magazine show "Sixty Minutes." Trial judge Robert Takasugi issued an order forbidding the broadcast of these tapes, which CBS successfully appealed. The law clerk and Flynt made money, and CBS boosted its ratings. Even though Judge Takasugi delayed the start of the trial for several months, the task of finding unbiased jurors was made substantially more difficult by this CBS broadcast.

At the other end of the trial a producer for the American Broadcasting Company's show "Good Morning America" made an effort to contact the jurors while they were deliberating the case in an effort to arrange interviews. Although he had previously issued such an order, Judge Takasugi was forced to repeat that all persons were forbidden to contact jurors while they were deliberating, and he added in case ABC did not understand that this order included attempts to establish interviews after the verdict. The United States attorney's office observed that this action might be viewed as jury tampering, a felony, and a defense lawyer characterized it as unethical, unprofessional, and irresponsible.

For both CBS and ABC the scoop and the audience that the scoop would attract were clearly more important than John

Delorean's Sixth Amendment rights. Even though the jury, after lengthy deliberations, found Delorean innocent on all charges, the possibility of conflict between the First and Sixth Amendments remains. As long as competition in news gathering and dissemination exists, pressure to engage in activities that may interfere with a defendant's rights will continue.

In the preceding pages we have seen how the acts and omissions of lawyers and judges have undermined the fair trial rights of defendants. The prosecution in the *Sheppard* case seemed eager to try the case in the press. The prosecution's withholding of evidence from the defense in the first Claus von Bülow trial may have been accidental. A recent example of a criminal case involving the rich and famous has been the Palm Beach, Florida, sexual battery (rape) case in which William Kennedy Smith (a member of the Massachusetts Kennedy family) was indicted. Shortly before the scheduled opening of the trial, Palm Beach county prosecutor Moira Lasch filed papers containing sworn statements from three women claiming that between 1983 and 1988 they had been sexually assaulted by Smith. The stated reason for the filing was to inform the defense of evidence that might be used against Smith. If the prosecution were only interested in proper notification of the defense, the statements could have been submitted under seal, or the defense could have been given an opportunity to obtain a court order sealing the documents.

The sworn statements by women who had never made criminal complaints against Smith for alleged actions in other jurisdictions three to eight years before the statements were filed had the predictable effect of poisoning the minds of the prospective jurors for the trial scheduled to begin less than a week after the filing. In addition there was real doubt in the legal community about the admissibility of these women's testimony when the case did come to trial, and in fact, the judge did not allow them to be used. After presenting survey evidence that showed a dramatic shift in public attitude against their client, Smith's lawyers were able to secure a postponement of his trial. Through the deliberate action of the prosecutor real damage had been done to Smith's right to an impartial jury to hear his case.

In another case decided by the United States Supreme Court on June 27, 1991, the pretrial statements of a defense lawyer were considered. Following the indictment of his client on criminal charges, Dominick Gentile held a press conference in which he proclaimed the innocence of his client and, in answer to reporters' questions, suggested that his client was the victim of a police conspiracy and cover-up. The Nevada Bar Association found Gentile guilty of violating Nevada Supreme Court Rule 177 that forbids lawyers from making statements that might have a "substantial likelihood of materially prejudicing" the outcome of a trial. Even though 1) Gentile's client was acquitted of all charges, 2) there is no evidence that the press conference influenced the trial in any way, and 3) apparently much of what Gentile said was true; the Nevada Supreme Court sustained the reprimand that the Bar Association had imposed.

When Gentile appealed this outcome to the United States Supreme Court, that court reversed in a closely divided decision. The five judge majority concluded that the rule as written and applied in this case was unconstitutionally vague and a violation of Gentile's First Amendment right of freedom of speech. Chief Justice William Rehnquist, writing for the four-judge minority, found no constitutional problem with the Nevada rule and its application to Dominick Gentile's press conference. He noted that forty-one states in addition to Nevada have similar rules for lawyers. Although one of those states is Florida, prosecutor Lasch is probably not subject to its application since she did her damage through a court filing rather than a press conference.

Appendix
Annotated Case List
Bibliography

Appendix
Protecting Confidential Information Sources

The basic purpose behind criminal investigation, rules concerning evidence, and the court trial process is to discover the truth as accurately and completely as possible. However, within our legal system this search for truth is not unlimited. In the Wayne Clapp murder case a central question was whether the statements made by the accused could be used against them. The Fifth Amendment to the Constitution states that no person "shall be compelled in any criminal case to be a witness against himself, . . ." Furthermore, the Fourth Amendment rules on search and seizure imply still other constitutional limitations on the truth discovery process.

A number of other limits are recognized in common law, legal traditions, and statutes. For example, it is generally accepted that a husband or wife cannot be forced to testify against his or her spouse. John Paul Stevenson's wife could not be forced to testify at his trials. Our society recognizes the special relationship that exists in a marriage and has decided that even criminal investigations and trials should not be allowed to interfere with that relationship. Priests, ministers, or rabbis cannot be asked to reveal what has been said to them in confidence by anyone. Here again it is generally recognized that it is more important to protect the central functions of organized religion than to gain the information that a forced revelation of the confidential communication would provide. Furthermore, most clergy would see an absolute ethical responsibility not to reveal such conversation.

A third generally recognized category of privileged communication—communication whose revelation cannot be required—is that between a doctor and patient. It has been concluded that the interests of society will best be served if nothing is allowed to inhibit free communication between these two. This attitude was demonstrated by the public reaction to the revelation that President Richard M. Nixon had ordered a break-in to a doctor's office in order to steal the psychiatric file of a patient being investigated by the government. The outrage was not just due to the fact that the act was illegal. The act was also morally reprehensible because it was a violation of the confidential doctor-patient relationship.

A fourth category of privileged communication is that between a lawyer and the lawyer's client. Obviously someone accused of a crime would find it virtually impossible to prepare a defense if the accused's lawyer could be required to divulge the contents of lawyer-client conversations. The widespread recognition that this privilege is right and proper can be seen in the public outcry that has resulted on those occasions when listening devices have been discovered in jailhouse conference rooms provided for lawyers and their clients. Here again it is not just that such bugging by the police is illegal. There is public recognition of a fundamental ethical violation as well.

While these situations in which there is a right to withhold evidence have widespread public and legal acceptance, there is still another category of privileged communication about which agreement is less complete—the right of a reporter to refuse to reveal confidential sources of information used to write a news story. It is not unusual for a reporter to be given a tip that leads to an important story. Such tips may deal with misconduct by some government employees or officials. The person giving the tip may work for the government agency involved. In this situation it is natural that the source would wish to remain secret because there would clearly be damaging consequences for the source if that source were revealed. In this situation it is clear that the willingness of a source to talk to a reporter depends upon assurance that the reporter will not disclose that source and conversation.

The value of confidentiality of news sources was well demonstrated in the series of stories that appeared in *The Washington Post* in 1972 and 1973 dealing with acts of misconduct by the national administration under the leadership and direction of President Nixon. The source, apparently a member of the Nixon administration, demanded that his identity be kept secret. The reporter involved would have been unable to give that guarantee if law enforcement officials could have forced the reporter to reveal his source. Without the information provided by the confidential source much of what came to be known as the Watergate scandal might never have been made public, and Richard Nixon might not have been forced to resign from office.

Representatives of the news media make the point that the activity of news reporting involves more than just writing and publishing stories. The process begins with and depends upon investigation and the discovery of facts. Without the uninhibited ability to investigate and gather facts, the freedom to write and publish guaranteed by the First Amendment would be severely restricted. Since a reporter's ability to protect the confidentiality of information sources is a significant element in the investigation and fact discovery process, reporters assert that their right to refuse to reveal confidential communication to anyone should be constitutionally protected by the First Amendment.

In 1972 the United States Supreme Court was asked to consider and rule on the proposition that reporters have a constitutional right to refuse to reveal information. Three different cases from three different parts of the country all dealing with this question were presented to the Court. Even though the facts of the three cases were very different, the Court combined them and issued one decision on the grounds that the issue involved was the same for all three.

Paul M. Branzburg was a young investigative reporter for *The Louisville* (Kentucky) *Courier-Journal* and the winner of several awards for his outstanding news stories. In 1969 and 1970 he wrote a series of stories dealing with drug traffic and use in Kentucky. These stories included details of the drug trade in Frankfort, the state capital, and an eyewitness description of the manufacture of hashish from marijuana in Louisville. One result of these stories was that Branzburg was twice called to testify before local grand juries investigating the criminal activities that his stories described. In both instances Branzburg refused to testify or reveal the names of the drug dealers about whom he wrote. After the second refusal, the district attorney brought Branzburg before a judge who, noting that all citizens have an obligation to testify about crimes they may have witnessed, ordered the reporter to give testimony. Branzburg pointed out that his stories which provided the public with important information about a significant social problem would have been impossible if he had not agreed to keep his sources secret. He again refused and was cited for contempt of court. Branzburg could have been sent to jail until he agreed to remove the contempt citation by answering the grand jury's questions. However, he appealed this contempt citation through the Kentucky state court system where the Kentucky Supreme Court eventually ruled against him. He then appealed to the United States Supreme Court on the grounds that the Kentucky court was violating his First Amendment rights as a reporter. The Supreme Court agreed to hear the case.

Earl Caldwell was a reporter with an impressive career. Since graduating from college, he had worked for progressively larger and more important papers leading to a position with *The New York Times*. Like Branzburg, his work had received awards including one from the Urban League. Being black, Caldwell had access to sources and was able to develop stories that a white reporter would have been unable to do. To make use of this special ability, *The Times* sent Caldwell to San Francisco to investigate and report on the Black Panther party which was becoming a significant force in the black community. Because the Panthers had had a number of negative experiences with the white community, particularly law enforcement officials, the group was very secretive and suspicious of outsiders. Caldwell was able to establish rapport with the group and gain their confidence. The result was a series of informative and insightful *Times* articles that helped to explain the Black Panther party to the public at large.

Information disclosed in the last few years has revealed that the Federal Bureau of Investigation, on orders from its director, J. Edgar Hoover, engaged in the illegal harassment of many black and other civil rights groups from the early 1960s until after Hoover's death in 1972. Among the targets for these illegal activities was the Black Panther party. As part of the harassment campaign a federal grand jury was impaneled in San Francisco in 1970 to investigate the Panthers even though the Justice Department had no evidence of any illegal activity. This type of investigation is sometimes called a "fishing expedition" because the prosecutor and jury have no idea what, if anything, they are going to find. Earl Caldwell was subpoenaed to appear before the grand jury bringing all his notes and any other materials dealing with the Panthers. Caldwell refused on the grounds that his very sensitive relationship with the Panthers would be destroyed if he even appeared. He would then be unable to write further about the Panthers. The Justice Department presented Caldwell's refusal to the federal court, and eventually the Ninth Circuit Court of Appeals ruled that Caldwell had a constitutional right to refuse to appear and testify based on the First Amendment. The Justice Department appealed this adverse decision to the United States Supreme Court, which agreed to hear the case.

In 1970 Paul Pappas was a television newsman working for

WTEV in New Bedford, Massachusetts, a racially mixed city to the south of Boston. In the course of his reporting Pappas had gotten to know some members of the local branch of the Black Panther party. This group of Panthers, like those in San Francisco, was, on the basis of its experience, extremely concerned about police harassment. Members of the group heard a rumor that the police intended to raid their party headquarters. For protection if anything should happen, the Panthers asked Pappas to spend the night with them in their headquarters, and Pappas accepted this invitation. When the local prosecutor heard about Pappas' visit, he subpoenaed Pappas to appear before a grand jury to tell everything that he had seen and heard that night. Pappas refused to testify on the grounds that the subpoena violated his First Amendment rights. This refusal became the basis for legal action that worked its way through the Massachusetts court system until the Massachusetts Supreme Court ruled that Pappas was required to testify. Pappas appealed this ruling to the United States Supreme Court, which once again agreed to hear the case.

On June 29, 1972, the Supreme Court handed down a single decision for all three cases. A closely divided Court decided against the claims of the reporters. The opinions for the five-justice majority was written by Justice Byron White. That opinion rejected the argument that the guarantees of the First Amendment extended to the protection of a reporter's sources. The majority declined to create what they saw as a new class of privileged communication and insisted that reporters have the same obligation as any other citizen to testify regarding criminal activities. The opinion failed to take into consideration the fact that of the three reporters only Paul Branzburg was known to have witnessed any criminal activity. One of the majority justices, Lewis Powell, wrote a concurring opinion in which he stated his view that in some cases reporters might have the right to refuse to testify. He said that in each case the judge should balance the needs of society and the obligation of any citizen to testify against the claim of privilege based on the First Amendment. Powell admonished judges to be sensitive to these First Amendment rights.

The four-justice minority produced two totally separate opinions. Justice William Douglas stated his view that reporters have an absolute right to refuse to testify and reveal sources based on the First Amendment. Justice Potter Stewart, writing for himself and Justices William Brennan and Thurgood Marshall, took the position that reporters can be required to testify if government is able to demonstrate compelling reasons for issuing the subpoena. It must be demonstrated that the information being sought is vital and unavailable through any other means. Justice Stewart concluded that this requirement had not been met in these three cases.

The Supreme Court's decision was both a disappointment to news media representatives and a surprise for two reasons. First, the Court had failed to differentiate among the three cases on the basis of the very different facts presented. Second, Justice William Rhenquist had participated in the decision. Traditionally members of the Supreme Court have demonstrated a strong ethical responsibility to avoid any appearance of impropriety. Even the remote possibility of a conflict of interest or any other special relationship to a case usually leads a justice to disqualify himself/herself as a matter of principle. For example, Justice Lewis Powell did not participate in the *Richmond Newspapers* case because he was aquainted with some of the people involved in the controversy.

Before his appointment to the Supreme Court by President Nixon in 1971, Justice Rhenquist had been an assistant attorney general in the Nixon Justice Department. In this capacity he had been directly involved in the issue of protecting reporters' sources. Rhenquist had represented the government's position against this First Amendment right in a public debate on the issue in Washington, D.C., in 1970. He was selected as spokesman for the government's view because of this role in drafting the Justice Department guidelines under which Earl Caldwell had been subpoenaed. Clearly Justice Rhenquist had prejudged the issue before it came to the Supreme Court, and it was expected that he would recognize his ethical obligation and decline to participate in these cases.

If Justice Rhenquist had not participated in these cases, the Supreme Court would have been evenly divided on the issue (because of Justice Powell's concurring opinion it can be speculated that the Court might have divided the cases and reached separate and different decisions in each case). When such an even split occurs, as it has in a number of cases, the decision of the lower court is sustained. In this instance the state court judgments against Branzburg and Pappas would have been upheld at the same time that the decision of the Ninth Circuit Court of Appeals in support of Earl Caldwell's First Amendment claim was sustained. Even this result, while unusual, would not have been unprecedented. For example, Justice William Douglas, because of a slight appearance of a possible conflict of interest, excused himself from participation in an obscenity case with the result that the film *I Am Curious—Yellow* was simultaneously found not obscene in the Second Circuit Court of Appeals and obscene in the Fourth Circuit Court of Appeals.

While the United States Supreme Court's decision of June 29, 1972, had decided the First Amendment constitutional issue of a reporter's right to protect sources, that decision had no effect on state laws on the subject. Such laws, known as shield laws, were in effect in a number of states prior to the Supreme Court's ruling and were enacted by several more states as a direct result of that controversial ruling. One state with such a law was California, and that law was cited by William Farr when he refused to reveal the sources of his news story during the Tate-LaBianca murders trial (note that Earl Caldwell was called to testify before a federal grand jury so the California state law did not apply).

The legal problems of William Farr arising out of the Tate-LaBianca murders trial illustrate well the issues involved in reporters' shield laws. Unlike New York law, which deals with the admissibility of evidence prior to trial (see the Wayne Clapp case), California state courts consider these challenges when they arise during the course of a trial, and the issue is decided while the jury is out of the courtroom. In the Tate-LaBianca case one of those who had presented testimony against the Manson group to the grand jury was Los Angeles County Jail inmate Virginia Graham. She told the grand jury about conversations she had with one of the defendants while they shared a jail cell. These conversations apparently dealt with plans by the Manson group to murder a number of other famous Hollywood celebrities. Lawyers for the defendants challenged the admissibility of Miss Graham's testimony at the trial on the grounds that it was hearsay evidence (as in John Paul Stevenson's murder trial) and asked for transcripts of her grand jury testimony in order to prepare their challenges. Judge Older, recognizing the sensational nature of the testimony, granted the defense request but admonished the lawyers as officers of the court not show the transcript or divulge its contents to anyone. The following day, October 9, 1971, the full transcript of the testimony appeared in a news story written by William Farr.

In reaction to this clear violation of the court's order Judge Older called each attorney before the bench and asked him as a sworn officer of the court whether he had provided the transcript to reporter Farr. Each one denied being the source. William Farr was then called before the court and asked to reveal his source. Farr cited the California shield law and on the basis of that law refused to answer Judge Older's questions. The entire matter was apparently closed after Judge Older listened to the defense arguments and sustained their objection to the admission of Miss Graham's testimony.

For Judge Older, however, the incident was not over. Shortly after the conclusion of the Tate-LaBianca murders trial, William Farr left the *Herald-Examiner* and took a position as a public relations consultant. In June 1972, Judge Older called Farr before him and ordered him to answer questions. The judge pointed out that since Farr was no longer a reporter, the California shield law no longer protected him. Farr still refused to answer questions, and Judge Older found him guilty of thirteen separate acts of contempt of court. Farr was sentenced to jail until he decided to purge himself of contempt by answering Judge Older's questions. Said Judge Older: "The purpose is not to punish Mr. Farr but to get the information as to who gave him those transcripts in violation of my order." On June 20, the judge recalled the defense lawyers and questioned them once more. Again, each one denied being the source of Farr's story. Finally on June 19, in an effort to purge himself of contempt, William Farr admitted that there had been more than one source for his story, that he had received three separate copies of the controversial transcript. Although he admitted that two transcript copies had come from defense lawyers, he still refused to name specifically any of the three sources. Farr also appealed his contempt of court convictions and after forty-six days in jail was released pending the outcome of that appeal. Finally on December 7, 1972, California Superior Court Judge Bernard Jefferson acquitted Farr of the contempt of court charges. Judge Jefferson's decision rested in part on his finding that there was no evidence that Farr had solicited the attorneys to violate their oath and give him copies of the transcript.

William Farr's legal problems seemed to be over. However, two of the defense lawyers filed a $24 million libel suit against him. They claimed to have been libeled by Farr by his refusal to tell Judge Older that they were not the ones who gave him the transcript copies. A California court finally dismissed that suit in 1983 because the two lawyers had not taken the steps necessary to bring it to trial. One last outcome of William Farr's ordeal was that California strengthened the protection of its shield law and made it part of the state constitution.

The problems of *The New York Times* and its reporter Myron Farber concerning protection of confidential sources illustrate the difficulties that have been created by the United States Supreme Court's decision that reporter-source communication is not privileged. Reporter Farber wrote a series of articles in 1979 dealing with some mysterious deaths in a New Jersey hospital nine years earlier. These stories suggested that the deaths were murders committed by a "Dr. X." An investigation by New Jersey law enforcement officials, apparently as a result of the newspaper stories, led to the indictment of Dr. Mario Jascalevich. He was accused of killing five patients in Riverdell Hospital in Oradell, New Jersey, in 1965 and 1966 by injecting them with fatal amounts of curare, a muscle relaxant.

The first sign of possible difficulties for Farber and *The New York Times* came at the outset of Dr. Jascalevich's trial on March 3, 1980. The doctor's lawyer asked that Farber be barred from the courtroom because he was a potential witness for the defense, and the judge agreed. Witnesses are normally excluded from the courtroom so that they will not be influenced by any of the other trial testimony. The surprise was that Farber, who apparently had no firsthand knowledge concerning the crimes, was included in the defense witness list. The court was then asked to order Farber to turn over all his notes and papers concerning the case to the defense. It was claimed that Farber had engaged in collusion with the New Jersey prosecutors and that these materials were essential in the preparation of Dr. Jascalevich's defense.

When the New Jersey trial court issued the order that Dr. Jascalevich had requested, Myron Farber, with the full support of his newspaper, refused to obey the court order. He cited the New Jersey state law giving him the right to protect his sources. That law says, in part:

> [A reporter] has a privilege to refuse to disclose, in any
> legal or quasi-legal proceeding . . . , any court, grand jury,
> petit jury, administrative agency, the Legislature or legisla-
> tive committee, or elsewhere,
>
>   a. The source . . . or person through whom any informa-
>   tion was procured . . . ; and
>   b. Any news or information obtained in the course of
>   pursuing his professional activities whether or not it is
>   disseminated.

The New Jersey Legislature had enacted this law in response to
the United States Supreme Court decision in the *Branzburg,
Caldwell, Pappas* case. The language of this statute clearly indicates that the intent was to guarantee total protection for all
reporter-source communication. However, the court pointed to a
defendant's right guaranteed in the New Jersey Constitution (ech-
oing the Sixth Amendment of the United States Constitution) to
secure evidence for his defense. The court ruled that the constitutional guarantee outweighed that of a state law and found Farber and *The New York Times* in contempt of court for their refusal
to supply the requested materials. Farber was sentenced to six
months in jail and until he supplied the material as ordered. *The
Times* was fined $100,000 plus $5,000 a day until it complied
with the court order. The court justified these severe sentences by
pointing to the fact that Dr. Jascalevich was on trial for murder
and being denied material that was claimed to be vital for his
defense.

While Farber was held in jail and the fines against *The Times*
mounted, the trial court decision and sentence were appealed
through the New Jersey courts. After twenty-six days of jail for
Farber and fines for *The Times*, the New Jersey Supreme Court
agreed to hear and decide the case. The court issued a stay pending its decision, which released Farber from jail and suspended
the fines against *The Times*.

The New Jersey Supreme Court took a little over a month to consider and rule on the appeal by Farber and *The New York Times*. On October 11, 1980, it ruled against Farber and *The Times* in a decision that restated the reasoning originally used by the trial court—Dr. Jascalevich's constitutional right to secure evidence that might aid in his defense outweighed the newspaper and reporter's right to withhold that evidence regardless of the clear statutory protection of the New Jersey law. Farber was returned to jail, and the daily fines against *The Times* began again.

Throughout this process Farber and *The Times* had addressed a series of appeals for relief to the United States Supreme Court. Individual justices had been asked to grant stays of the sentence of the New Jersey court. While stays of a day or two had been granted, no real relief was provided. The entire United States Supreme Court was also asked to consider the case after the New Jersey Supreme Court issued its decision. The United States Supreme Court refused to accept the case. While the reason for refusal was not stated, it was probable that the Court considered the constitutional issues involved settled by the *Branzburg, Caldwell, Pappas* case.

Meanwhile, the murder trial of Dr. Jascalevich went forward. Both sides presented their cases to the jury. Less than two weeks after Farber was jailed for the second time the jury returned its verdict. It found Dr. Jascalevich innocent of all the charges against him. This conclusion of the trial meant that Myron Farber and *The New York Times* were no longer in contempt of court since the information they withheld was no longer needed. Farber was freed from jail. The accumulation of fines against *The Times* ended at $285,000. While the New Jersey courts eventually decided to refund most of the fine paid by *The New York Times*, no one could restore the days that Myron Farber spent in prison.

Although the particular case of Myron Farber, *The New York Times*, Dr. Mario Jascalevich, and the State of New Jersey had been resolved, the issues remain. Even though the legislature of

New Jersey sought to provide absolute protection for reporter-source communication, the courts balanced that protection against the constitutional rights of a criminal defendant and found it wanting. Here the conflict was a direct one between freedom of the press and the right to a fair trial in which a fair trial was viewed as more important. The outcome of the trial proved that the information that Farber was withholding was not vital. However, if Dr. Jascalevich had been found guilty, the refusal of Farber and *The Times* to provide the requested information would seem to establish a clear basis for a mistrial or a reversal of the jury's decision on appeal. Farber and *The Times* would still be in contempt of court. Under these circumstances how high a price would Myron Farber and *The New York Times* be willing to pay to maintain the principle that reporter-source communication is privileged?

In the book that he had planned to write on the case from the outset of his involvement with it and which was finally published in 1982 under the title *Somebody Is Lying*, Farber claimed that the defense request for all his material was, to use his word, a game. Farber stated that the defense wanted a refusal to give them grounds to appeal an unfavorable verdict. Whatever the motives of all those involved, the Jascalevich murder trial and the legal problems of Myron Farber and *The New York Times* demonstrate once again that there are no final answers, that the perfect balance between free press and fair trial has yet to be found.

Annotated Case List

The crimes and trials that have been described in the preceding pages have resulted in a number of decisions and opinions by courts that have reviewed the work of the original trial courts. Reference has been made to these decisions and opinions. The purpose here is to identify the published court opinions in these cases and a selected few others so that those interested can read further. Each case is listed by its formal name with a citation number which identifies the volume number, the work, and the first page number of the opinion. A citation "123 U.S. 456" would indicate that in volume 123 of the *United States Reports* the opinion of the United States Supreme Court in this case begins on page 456.

Cases discussed in this book

1. *Sheppard v. Maxwell, Warden*, 384 U.S. 333 (1966)
   This United States Supreme Court opinion is the one written by Justice Tom Clark in the suit claiming that Sam Sheppard was wrongfully imprisoned brought against the warden of the Ohio prison where Sheppard was being held.
2. *Nebraska Press Association v. Stuart*, 427 U.S. 539 (1976)
   In the Kellie murders case the Nebraska Press Association filed a suit against the judge who had issued the order that forbade publication of specific details of the crime.
3. *Gannett v. DePasquale*, 443 U.S. 368 (1979)
   In the Wayne Clapp case the Gannett Company brought suit

against Judge DePasquale in response to his decision to close the pretrial hearing in this case.

4. *Richmond Newspapers v. Virginia,* 448 U.S. 555 (1980)
   This opinion is the result of the suit brought by Richmond Newspapers over the decision to close John Paul Stevenson's fourth murder trial.

5. *Estes v. Texas,* 381 U.S. 532 (1965)
   Billy Sol Estes, a financial wheeler-dealer with apparent connections to important Texas politicians, was indicted on a variety of financial misconduct charges. One of his major scams was borrowing very large sums of money using non-existent tanks of liquid fertilizer as security. This case was given extensive nationwide coverage, publicity that led to a change of venue for the trial to east Texas some 500 miles from the Pecos area where the crimes had been committed. To satisfy the substantial public interest in this trial being held in a remote area, the trial judge allowed live radio and television broadcast of pretrial activities. At one point twelve separate television cameras were in the courtroom. Estes appealed his conviction on the grounds that this broadcasting violated his Sixth Amendment rights. The majority of the United States Supreme Court agreed and granted Estes a new trial. The several opinions in this case made it unclear whether all broadcasting or just the broadcasting in this case violated the Sixth Amendment.

6. *Chandler v. Florida,* 449 U.S. 560 (1981)
   Sixteen years after *Estes* the United States Supreme Court clarified its position on broadcasting. In this case two Miami Beach police officers' on-duty burglary activities were accidentally overheard by a ham radio operator. At the time of the officers' trial Florida was experimenting with television in the courtroom. The officers objected to the broadcasting and appealed their conviction on the ground that their right to a fair trial was automatically violated by the

broadcasting. A unanimous United States Supreme Court rejected this reading of *Estes* and held that the unobtrusive broadcasting that modern technology permits does not violate the Sixth Amendment.

7. *Branzburg v. Hayes, U.S. v. Caldwell, Pappas v. Massachusetts,* 408 U.S. 665 (1972)

This opinion is the conclusion of the United States Supreme Court in the three different situations where reporters were claiming the right to protect their sources. An interesting contrast can be found in the opinion of the United States Ninth Circuit Court of Appeals in the *Caldwell* case (*Caldwell v. U.S.,* 434 F.2d 1081 [9th Cir. 1970]).

8. *Farr v. Superior Court of Claifornia,* 22 Cal. App. 3d 60 (1972)

This opinion deals with William Farr's contempt of court jail sentence for refusing to reveal the source of grand jury testimony that he received and published during the Manson murder trial. A second opinion that finally freed Farr from the possibility of further jail time is *In re William T. Farr,* 64 Cal. App. 3d 605 (1976).

9. *In re Farber,* 78 N.J. 259 (1978)

This reference is to the opinion of the New Jersey Supreme Court that upheld the contempt penalties against Myron Farber and *The New York Times* in the Jascalevich murder trial.

Other Important Free Press/Fair Trial Cases

1. *State of Maryland v. Baltimore Radio Show,* 338 U.S. 912 (1950)

Prior to a murder trial in Baltimore a local radio station broadcast a program that stated that the accused had confessed, had a long prior criminal record, and had, when taken to the scene of the crime, reenacted the murder. The trial court found the radio station in contempt of court for broadcasting a program that so prejudiced the fair trial rights of the defendant. This contempt citation was struck down by the Maryland appeals court, and the state appealed to the United States Supreme Court, which refused to hear the case. This citation is to that refusal to which Justice Felix Frankfurter attached a long memo in dissent. The memo provides an excellent discussion of the way in which the British system uses the contempt of court power to protect criminal defendants from prejudicial publicity.

2. *Sheperd v. Florida,* 341 U.S. 50 (1951)

This case involved the reversal of the conviction of four blacks. While the basic reason given by the United States Supreme Court majority for this reversal was the exclusion of all blacks from the grand jury that indicted the four, three justices also noted extensive prejudicial pretrial publicity including reports that confessions had been made.

3. *Irvin V. Dowd,* 366 U.S. 717 (1961)

In this opinion the United States Supreme Court considered the trial of Leslie "Mad Dog" Irvin and, for the first time, reversed a conviction on the basis of prejudicial pretrial publicity. Leslie Irvin, a recent prison parolee, was arrested in Evansville, Indiana, on a burglary charge. Within a few days the county prosecutor issued a press release stating that Irvin had confessed to six recent murders in the area. The local media, with the co-operation of law enforcement agencies, reported extensively and prejudicially about the case. Irvin was granted a change of venue but only to an adjoining county. During the voir dire examination of prospective jurors, 370 of the 430 persons called to serve indicated that they believed that Irvin was guilty. In fact, eight of the jurors finally selected admitted to having formed an opinion about Irvin's guilt. This evidence from the trial record led the United States Supreme Court to order a new trial for Irvin in a locality that had not been inflamed by prejudicial publicity. Retired in a nonprejudicial atmosphere, Leslie Irvin was once again found guilty of the six murders.

4. *Rideau v. Louisiana,* 373 U.S. 73 (1963)

In this case the police in Lake Charles, Louisiana, had allowed local television station KLPC to film a twenty-minute conversation in the jail between Wilbert Rideau and the sheriff of Calcasieu parish. In the course of this conversation Rideau admitted robbing the Lake Charles bank, kidnapping three bank employees, and killing one of them. Over a period of three days KLPC broadcast this filmed conversation three times. The estimated audience for these broadcasts was 97,000 in a county with a total population of 150,000. Rideau's attorney requested a change of venue arguing that his client could not receive a fair trial in the community where this confession had been broadcast. While the trial court refused this request, the United States Supreme Court reversed Rideau's subsequent conviction and ordered that he be given a new trial in a jurisdiction where the broadcasts had not been seen.

5. *Gentile v. State Bar of Nevada,* 59 L.W. 4858 (1991)

In this case a closely divided court rescinded the reprimand of a defense lawyer by the Nevada Bar Association. The lawyer had held a press conference in which he proclaimed the innocence of his client. The Bar Association said that the press conference violated Nevada court rules that forbid statements that have a "substantial likelihood of materially prejudicing" a trial outcome. The Supreme Court majority concluded that this rule as applied in this case violated the lawyer's freedom of speech.

Bibliography

BOOKS

Advisory Committee on Fair Trial and Free Press. *Approved Draft Standards Relating to Fair Trial and Free Press.* New York: American Bar Association, 1968.

American Bar Association Legal Advisory Committee on Fair Trial and Free Press. *Preliminary Draft Proposed Court Procedure for Fair Trial-Free Press Judicial Restrictive Orders.* New York: American Bar Association, 1975.

——. *Recommended Court Procedure to Accommodate Rights of Fair Trial and Free Press.* New York: American Bar Association, 1976.

American Society of Newspaper Editors. *Free Press and Fair Trial.* Washington, D.C.: American Newspaper Publishers Association Foundation, 1987.

Association of the Bar of the City of New York, Special Committee on Radio and Television. *Radio, Television and the Administration of Justice.* New York: Columbia University Press, 1965.

Association of the Bar of the City of New York, Special Committee on Radio and Television, and the Administration of Justice. *Freedom of the Press and Fair Trial.* New York: Columbia University Press, 1967.

Bailey, F. Lee. *The Defense Never Rests.* New York: Stein and Day, 1971.

Barron, Jerome, and C. Thomas Dienes. *Handbook of Free Speech and Free Press.* Boston: Little, Brown & Co., 1979.

Bugliosi, Vincent, and Curt Gentry. *Helter Skelter: The True Story of the Manson Murders.* New York: W. W. Norton 1974.

Bush, Chilton R., ed. *Free Press and Fair Trial: Some Dimensions of the Problem.* Athens: University of Georgia Press, 1971.

Dershowitz, Alan. *Reversal of Fortune: Inside the von Bülow Case.* New York: Random House, 1986.

Dickler, Gerald. *Man on Trial—History-Making Trials from Socrates to Oppenheimer.* New York: Doubleday & Co., 1962.

Farber, Myron. *Somebody Is Lying.* New York: Doubleday & Co., 1982.

Frank, Jerome. *Courts on Trial—Myth and Reality in American Justice.* Princeton, N.J.: Princeton University Press, 1949.

Freedman, Warren. *Press and Media Access to the Criminal Courtroom.* New York: Quorum Books, 1988.

Friendly, Alfred, and Ronald Goldfarb. *Crime and Publicity.* New York: Random House, 1968.

Gillmor, Donald M. *Judicial Restraints on the Press.* Columbia: University of Missouri Freedom of Information Center, 1974.

Graber, Doris A. *Crime News and the Public.* New York: Praeger Publishers, 1980.

Hariman, Robert, ed. *Popular Trials: Rhetoric, Mass Media, and the Law.* Tuscaloosa: University of Alabama Press, 1990.

Hays, Arthur Garfield. *Trial by Prejudice.* New York: Covici-Friede, 1933.

Hemmer, Joseph J. *Communication Under the Law, Vol. 2: Journalistic Freedom.* Metuchen, N.J.: Scarecrow Press, 1980.

Hiss, Alger. *In the Court of Public Opinion.* New York: Alfred A. Knopf, 1957.

Holmes, Paul. *The Sheppard Murder Case*. New York: David McKay Co., 1961.

Hughes, Helen M. *News and the Human Interest Story*. Chicago: University of Chicago Press, 1940.

Judicial Administration Division. *Courts and Community*. Salt Lake City: American Bar Association, 1973.

Kalven, Harry, and Hans Zeisel. *The American Jury*. Boston: Little, Brown & Co., 1966.

Kaplin, John, and Jon R. Waltz. *The Trial of Jack Ruby*. New York: The Macmillan Co., 1965.

Lofton, John. *Justice and the Press*. Boston: Beacon Press. 1966.

Morris, Richard B. *Fair Trial—Fourteen Who Stood Accused from Anne Hutchison to Alger Hiss*. New York: Alfred A. Knopf, 1952.

Patterson, Haywood, and Earl Conrad. *Scottsboro Boy*. New York: Doubleday & Co., 1950.

Schuetz, Janice, and Kathryn Holmes Snedaker. *Communication and Litigation: Case Studies of Famous Trials*. Carbondale: Southern Illinois University Press, 1988.

Shaw, Donald, and Maxwell McCombs. *The Emergence of American Political Issues: The Agenda-Setting Function of the Press*. St. Paul, Minn.: West Publishing Co., 1977.

Simons, Howard, and Joseph Califano. *The Media and the Law*. New York: Praeger Publishers, 1976.

Waller, George. *Kidnap*. New York: Pocket Books, 1962.

Wigmore, John H. *A Kaleidoscope of Justice—Containing Authentic Accounts of Trial Scenes from All Times and Climes*. Washington, D.C.: Washington Law Book Co., 1941.

ARTICLES

Babcock, Barbara Allen. "Voir Dire: preserving 'Its Wonderful Powers.'" *Stanford Law Review,* 27 (1975), 545–65.

Gerald, J. Edward. "Press-Bar Relationships: Progress Since Sheppard and Reardon." *Journalism Quarterly,* 47 (1970), 223–32.

Giglio, Ernest D. "Free Press-Fair Trial in Britain and America." *Journal of Criminal Justice,* 10 (1982), 341–58.

Hofer, Stephen. "The Fallacy of Farber: Failure to Acknowledge the Constitutional Newsman's Privilege in Criminal Cases." *Journal of Criminal Law and Criminology,* 70 (1979), 299–336.

Keefe, Arthur J. "The Boner Called Gannett." *Amerian Bar Association Journal,* 66 (1980), 227–30.

Kielbowicz, Richard B. "The Story Behind the Adoption of the Ban on Courtroom Cameras." *Judicature,* 63 (June–July 1979), 14–23.

Kline, F. Gerald, and Paul H. Jess. "Prejudicial Publicity: Its Effect on Law School Mock Juries." *Journalism Quarterly,* 43 (1966), 113–16.

Landau, Jack C. "Fair Trial and Free Press: A Due Process Proposal." *American Bar Association Journal,* 62 (1976), 55–64.

Minow, Newton N., and Fred H. Cate. "Who Is an Impartial Juror in an Age of Mass Media?" *The American University Law Review,* 40 (1991), 631–64.

"Protective Orders Against the Press and the Inherent Powers of the Courts." *Yale Law Journal,* 87 (1977), 342–71.

Riley, Sam. "Pre-Trial Publicity: A Field Study." *Journalism Quarterly.* 50 (1973), 17–23.

Sack, Robert D. "Principle and *Nebraska Press Association v. Stuart.*" *Stanford Law Review,* 29 (1977), 411–30.

"Sequestration: A Possible Solution to the Free Press-Fair Trial Dilemma." *American University Law Review,* 23 (1974), 923–57.

Simon, Rita J. "Does the Court's Decision in *Nebraska Press Association* Fit the Research Evidence on the Impact on

Jurors of News Coverage?" *Stanford Law Review,* 29 (1977), 515–28.

————. "Murders, Juries and the Press." *Transaction,* 3 (May–June 1966), 40–42.

Stephenson, D. G., Jr. "Fair Trial—Free Press: Rights in Continuing Conflict." *Brooklyn Law Review,* 46 (1979), 39–66.

Trager, Robert, and Harry W. Stonecipher. "Gag Orders: An Unresolved Dilemma." *Journalism Quarterly,* 55 (1978), 231–40.

Warren, Robert S., and Jeffrey M. Abell. "Free Press-Fair Trial, the Gag Order: A California Aberration." *Southern California Law Review,* 45 (1972), 51–99.